Natural FOOD RECIPES

FOR *Healthy* **DOGS**

CAROL BOYLE

Howell Book House
New York

Visit our website at http://www.naturaldogfood.com

Howell Book House
A Simon and Schuster Macmillan Company
1633 Broadway
New York, NY 10019

MACMILLAN is a registered trademark of Macmillan, Inc.

Library of Congress Cataloging-in-Publication Data

Boyle, Carol, 1945–
    Natural food recipes for the healthy dog / Carol Boyle.
        p.   cm.
    Includes bibliographical references and index.
    ISBN 0-87605-584-6
        1. Dogs—Food—Recipes.   2. Dogs—Health   3. Natural foods.
    I. Title
    SF427.4.B69   1997
    636.7'085—dc21   97-8263
                                                      CIP

Manufactured in the United States of America

10 9 8 7 6 5 4 3 2

Book Design by designLab, Seattle

Contents

This book is dedicated to Patou.

Patou at 14 years, 3 months. (Photo by Karen Reiter)

Foreword

I don't remember when it was exactly that I met Carol, her husband Ed, and the remarkable Patou, but I do remember my reaction when I incredulously repeated my question about Patou's age, "He's *how old?!* What are you feeding this dog that he's in such superb shape?"

Carol, in her soft sweet way, replied that she cooked for Patou, to which I said, "I cook for my dogs, too, but they don't look this good and they're significantly younger." Carol proceeded to share her secrets for dog lasagna and other goodies, and I quickly realized that Patou eats a far better diet than I do. She left me with copies of her recipes and the encouragement to share them with other concerned dog owners. So began a friendship with the Boyle family that has led to this Foreword.

I had a semblance of nutrition in veterinary college, although I consider my true education in canine nutrition began when I met Wendy Volhard and was introduced to "Natural Diet." As much as I love and respect Wendy, I can't keep all the ingredients straight, to which she patiently shakes her head, and says, "Now, Sue Ann . . . " and respects me for my veterinary talents and loves me in spite of my inability to cope with the intricacies of "Natural Diet." (As an aside, dogs on "Natural Diet" look great and live long, healthy lives, but my own dogs find morning oatmeal insulting and my Princess dog doesn't eat liver unless it's sautéed in butter with Pernod and *fines herbes*.)

What Carol has done for those who want to cook for their canine companions and are confused as to where to start, is to formulate a dietary plan that is well-balanced and more importantly, *simple:* simple to shop for, simple to cook and simple to encourage your dogs to eat. (The Princess loves canine lasagna, the more garlic and oregano the better.)

Although Patou is a sparkling example of the health benefits of Carol's sensible approach to the canine culinary arts, and that in itself is encouragement to try "Boyle cuisine," my favorite aspect is sharing time with my dogs in our favorite place, the kitchen, doing what we all like to do best, and that's cooking and eating good food. Bon appetite!

Sue Ann Lesser, DVM, CAC
South Huntington, NY
September, 1996

Acknowledgments

This book could not have been written without the encouragement and help of my most ardent supporter, my husband Ed. Years ago, his questions about dogs and natural foods sent me on a path of discovery that changed the way I looked at dogs' nutritional needs. It was with his encouragement that I started this project, and finally finished it with his support.

Special thanks to my mother, Domicella (Dommie), who gave me a love of food as well as my first lessons in cooking, and to my father, Frank J. Brescher, who taught me early in life that girls can do anything that they make up their minds up to do.

And thanks to all of those special people who gave of their precious time to make this book happen. Thanks to Sue Ann Lesser, DVM, CAC, who so thoroughly reviewed the chapter on the performance dog. And to Charles Schenck, DVM, for reviewing those chapters on old and sick dogs. It is Dr. Lesser who adjusts our 14-year-old Patou regularly, and Dr. Schenck who ministers to his other veterinary needs. Thanks also to Anne Boles, who reviewed the puppy chapter and so graciously provided the photographs of her Belgian Sheepdogs doing therapy work.

Thanks to Stephanie Staszak for the photographs of her Portugese Water Dog, and to Bill McCaffery for his pictures of Henry, the Bernese Mountain Dog. And special thanks to Karen Reiter, who photographed Patou winning "Oldest Pyr in Fun Match" on October 5, 1996. He was 14 years, three months old.

I have been very lucky to have a wonderful friend and Great Pyrenees devotee in Michelle Nemiroff. Michelle gave me my first copy of the Pitcairn book that helped jump start my natural food program. She continually provides new and refreshing outlooks, and challenges me with exciting and alternate views of traditional human medical and canine veterinary care.

And last, but most important, I have to thank Patou. He instinctively knew what was good for him. I only responded to him. I followed his lead, and as a result could keep him well and healthy all of these years. What I learned and put into practice in the way of natural foods could never have happened without him. He, and his successes with natural foods, are the reasons this book was written.

Keystones for a Natural Diet

Provide a clean, healthy water supply.

Water is the most important ingredient in the well-being of any animal. An animal can live for days, if not weeks, without food, but not without water.

Make certain that water is readily available and that it is as pure as possible. Test your tap water for any possible contaminants and use the appropriate filtering mechanism to filter them out. It is critical that your water supply is safe and pure, for both the canine and human members of your family.

Eat at the bottom of the food chain.

Emphasize those foods that are at the bottom of the food chain, the grains and vegetables. Those foods higher on the chain are also higher in fats, pesticides and other pollutants. Three quarters of the volume of food should be vegetables and carbohydrates/grains. Only one quarter should be high quality protein.

Cook all meats, seafood, poultry and eggs.

No meats, seafood, poultry or eggs are to be fed raw. You cannot adequately monitor this part of the food supply. Do not jeopardize your animal's health.

Wash all produce well to decrease pesticide consumption.

Wash all produce, even if it is organically grown, in cold water to cover. You may choose to add half a teaspoon of all-purpose bleach to each gallon of water. Soak for 10 minutes and rinse well. Then soak in clean rinse water for 10 minutes.

Seek variety in all things.
While your dog may choose not to eat a particular food, do not eliminate any group of foods from the diet.

Balance the variety with moderation.
Do not feed any one specific food or group of foods to the exclusion of the others.

Keep it simple, keep it fresh.
A meal of chicken, rice and broccoli should consist of just that.

Keep an open mind.
Ideas and information about different food benefits and characteristics grow and change daily. Realize that what you learned five years ago may not be applicable today. Listen, study and learn. And *question everything.*

PART I

Going Natural

Chapter 1

Why a Natural Food Diet?

My approach to canine nutrition may be considered radical to many people. Very simply, I share my meals with our dog. Our dog is a member of the family, and I make certain that the foods I provide for all my family are nutritious and healthy. This care is an extension of my love and my concern for their well-being. It just happens that part of my family is canine.

It was not always like this. For years I had been the concerned but traditional dog owner, reading commercial dog food labels, comparing ingredients and breakdowns by protein and fat, and so on. I had established a fairly normal combination of a high-quality kibble and meat mix. The dogs ate it, so everything was fine. It was 1987, and my husband Ed and I shared our lives with two Great Pyrenees.

Then things changed. This turning point is burned into my memory.

It was an early fall evening, and Ed and I were enjoying the quiet beauty of the river that flows gently past our backyard. Happily settled near us were our Pyrs, Cher and her son Patou. Ed began wishing out loud for the ability to freeze this moment in time and prolong the good health of our two dogs. They were the last dogs of our breeding program, the fourth and fifth generations from our kennel, which had been plagued with bad luck and heartache. The average lifespan for a Great Pyrenees is seven to nine years. We were pushing the odds with Cher, who had just turned 10. Patou was five.

That evening, Ed asked me a series of questions that would set me on a path of discovery and changed the way I looked at things forever. He asked, quite simply:

1 What is the difference between a dog's body and a human's body? We both have blood, muscles, require oxygen, and so on.

2 What kind of nutrition would be required to provide "optimum" growth and maintenance for a dog?

3 Are we doing the best for our dogs by feeding them commercially manufactured and processed foods, which we try to avoid eating ourselves?

I responded to each of his questions in order:

1 I don't think there is that much difference. We are both animals, omnivorous mammals, both with physiologies that include a circulatory system, digestive system, musculoskeletal system, hormonal (endocrine) system, and so on. (All things I had once known but needed to relearn.)

2 I'm sure we can find out (I prematurely boasted).

3 Put in those terms, of course not (I, the fresh vegetable advocate, replied indignantly).

As the primary caregiver, chief cook and bottle washer, I rose to the challenge. Was I, indeed, doing the best I could for my dogs by feeding them canned meat mix combined with dry kibble?

I read anything I could find on canine nutrition and talked at length with my veterinarians. A friend, knowing of my search, sent me a copy of *Dr. Pitcairn's Complete Guide to Natural Health for Dogs and Cats* (Rodale Press, 1982). Many of my questions about nutrition continued to remain unanswered, and new questions about the pet food industry arose at an alarming rate. What started out as mere curiosity had taken on the trappings of a quest.

When we built our kennel addition in the '70s, I had allocated space to buy dog food in bulk. I quickly learned that in the summer I had to limit the amounts that were purchased. Within two weeks the food would become moldy and buggy. I cannot remember when this stopped being a problem, but it did. In fact, after I read Pitcairn's book, I placed some of the kibble I had in a glass jar on my kitchen counter. It remained there for four years before I threw it away. Nothing grew on it or in it.

If lower forms of life could not exist on this food, how could I expect my dear dogs to thrive on it? The word *preservatives* took on a whole new meaning. Perhaps if the word had been pesticides, I might have been quicker on the uptake.

Just when I started feeding our dogs natural food, Cher began passing extremely dark urine. A number of tests were performed. The diagnosis was liver failure. The prognosis was grim. My veterinarian recommended a low-fat diet: "Check the labels for fat content," he said. Fortunately, I had complete control over her diet, so reducing the fat content was not difficult.

Cher seemed to do well for more than a year (much longer than the two to three months that my veterinarian had anticipated), then took a turn for the worse. We lost her on a snowy February day. She was 11.

Then there was one.

Here Patou at age nine takes his friend Alexandra Brown for a walk on an island in Maine. (Photo by Ed Boyle)

Over time, Patou has done marvelously well on this diet. And Patou is 14 now. He has been eating "human" food for over nine years. What does he eat? Mostly, whatever we eat.

I love to cook and have always had a natural curiosity about foods and nutrition. Years ago I edited a book on holistic medicine. This caused me to look at food in a new way. If our bodies are a chemical furnace, the types of food we eat (the chemicals) will have a direct (positive or negative) effect on the maintenance and upkeep of that body. And we consume those chemicals daily, 365 days a year. So do our pets.

For years, research focused on the foods that were "bad for you" and diseases associated with eating too much of a specific food or food group. I was always fascinated with the other side of the coin: the healing qualities of certain herbs and foods. Many of the drugs we use today came from plants, and are now created synthetically. Scientists are just beginning to scratch the surface on other positive aspects of foods. Vitamins are only part of the story. We all are aware of the benefits of anti-oxidants, fiber, omega-3 fatty acids, phytochemicals and acidophilus cultures in yogurt. Some foods are simply good for you.

Because many foods actually benefit the body and improve the way it functions, we all should concentrate on these foods. At the same time, many of the positive aspects of food are still not known. Therefore, we cannot ignore any foods or food groups.

Years ago I developed a personal theory of nutrition that I have tried to follow. I call it The Scatter-Shot Theory: If you eat a little bit of everything and do not overindulge in anything, you will eat a nutritionally sound diet.

This theory, coupled with the fact that my husband has a low tolerance for salt and I have a low tolerance for fat, has caused our diet to evolve into a low-sodium, low-fat one. Forget eating at fast food chains and many restaurants. Eating out has become a rare occasion. Most of our meals are prepared at home, by us.

How does this apply to our dog's diet? Simple. We all eat the same kinds of food. I shop the edge of the supermarket and concentrate on "good for you" foods; fresh fruits and vegetables, fresh meat, dairy products and breads. We eat very few processed foods.

While no one can or will guarantee fresh human food 100 percent, we know it is better than dog food. I know that the food is fresh, hope it has been handled properly en route to the markets and has a minimum amount of preservatives (or pesticides), because all of the food is geared for human consumption.

And while I cannot guarantee that Patou's diet alone yields the optimum nutrition that started me on this route, I know that I am not filling his body with pesticides, or feeding him rancid or tainted food. While this may not be the sole or total solution to optimum health, we at least know that this food regimen is not part of the problem.

I do not consider myself an expert on canine nutrition. All of my evidence is anecdotal, from personal experience, over a period of time. And although I have no formal training in canine nutrition, I am a great reader, a great observer, and I have an open mind. And in my "unbiased opinion" Patou has done marvelously well on this diet.

Patou is a French dog, and his absolutely favorite food is freshly baked French bread. He will eat this before any other kind of food, including meat.

He also likes vegetables. He loves the crunch of fresh string beans—raw. If he knows I have fresh beans, he will not leave me alone until I rinse a few and give them to him as an appetizer. He gets more cooked with dinner.

I do not pretend to know what nutrients from vegetables are more readily available to him in a raw or cooked state, so I make certain each week he gets some of each (once again, the Scatter-Shot Theory).

Springtime finds Patou and the rest of the family craving fresh green vegetables. This usually means asparagus sautéed in water until it is tender and crisp. Patou will eat as much asparagus as he is offered. Broccoli, Brussels spouts, corn, eggplant, white and sweet potatoes and all kinds of winter and summer squash are eagerly consumed.

Feeding your adult dog is like feeding another adult family member, so make the meatloaf a little bigger. Buy a turkey that weighs a little more. Capons are great for Sunday dinners, with leftovers for later in the week. My canine lasagna became a family favorite when my husband thought it was his dinner and microwaved it. Turnabout is fair play. Dog food can become people food.

Patou weighs about 103 pounds and stands 27 inches at the shoulder. He consumes approximately 1,200 calories a day in the summer and slightly more in the winter. In his prime he would only eat one meal—a large dinner. Since he turned 12, he has looked for a second meal at breakfast. I just prepare one large dinner and put part of it in the refrigerator to be served the next morning at breakfast, microwaved just enough to bring it up to room temperature.

While many dogs prefers their food unsalted, they usually still love fat. French fries rank right up there with green beans, and Patou (like Ed and I) loves good Chinese take-out and pizza. All in moderation (the Scatter-Shot Theory again!).

THE PROBLEM WITH SALT

I had always been told that salt is not good for people, particularly people who are "salt sensitive." No one could ever adequately explain what the specific problem was with salt, until a friend of mine had a dog with hypothyroidism.

Junior was a beautiful, wonderfully laid-back male Great Pyrenees. He was from one of our first litters, and we marked him early on as a "keeper." However, once he met Michelle and Alfred Nemiroff, he was in love with them. And it was mutual.

And at approximately eight years of age he developed hypothyroidism. He was being treated by a veterinarian in Albany, and I made the trip with Michelle on a couple of occasions. This veterinarian taught me about the problem with salt.

There is a direct relationship between salt and water. The more salt an animal consumes, the more water is retained in the organs of the body, including the blood. The blood becomes diluted. In order for the tissues in the body to receive the same amount of oxygen they would from undiluted blood, the heart has to pump harder, to move the blood faster. This increases the blood pressure as it passes through the circulatory system, and forces the heart to work harder.

Salt, per se, is not bad for you. It is the effect it has on the fluids in your system that wreaks havoc.

All the way through this book, I cook with a minimum of salt, preferring to allow you the option of adding salt at the table. I use sea salt and Kosher salt. I keep a small jar of Kosher salt next to my sugar container. In trying new recipes that require direct measurements, I will 1) reduce the required amount by a half, and 2) use Kosher salt which, because of its larger granules, measures differently. A tablespoon of Kosher salt is more like two teaspoons of regular salt.

You will discover that the salt will probably not be missed. And where the food tastes a little flat, add the salt at the table. I have found that on the few occasions that I have forgotten to add salt during the cooking, it was OK when the meal was hot, but missed terribly when it was cold.

A little salt enhances food and brings out its flavor. But it is too easy to over-salt food, and this condiment, like fat, becomes addictive. More is better as your taste buds become numbed to this seasoning. After you have withdrawn, or lowered your salt intake, you will find the tingle on the lips and the tingle on the tongue an irritating sensation.

While our dogs have always loved their fat, they seem to prefer their food unsalted. While many foods may taste slightly flat without the addition of salt, you will find that many times the salt actually masks the natural sweetness of foods, particularly vegetables.

The following foods contain levels of salt high enough that they can undermine your recipes. When using these products, do not add any additional salt until the very end of the recipe. Then taste and correct the seasonings if necessary.

- Soy sauce
- Teriyaki sauce
- Canned tomato sauce
- Canned soups
- Prepared pasta sauces
- Canned broth (both chicken and beef)
- Bouillon cubes (very high)
- Parmesan and Romano cheese
- MSG

The low-fat diet has not adversely affected Patou's coat. Great Pyrenees have a non-oily coat that never shines. His coat, however, is abundant and silvery, and his skin is healthy. With friends' dogs that have been on similar diets, the results have been the same.

In fact, there have been no long-term negative side effects to this diet. And there have been some very positive ones. For example, all of our dogs always ate grass and then regurgitated it. I never read a really specific reason for this, but I do accept the fact that their bodies crave something in that green plant. Patou has not eaten grass since he has been eating fresh vegetables on this diet.

When I switched Patou and Cher to home prepared food, I went the whole way. It worked well for me and I am thrilled with the results. But if you cannot or will not totally eliminate commercial foods, consider adding fresh foods to your dog's dinner. I'm not talking about scraps. If you were going to throw it in the garbage, that's probably where it belongs. And I'm not talking about the usual "home cooked" fast foods or packaged cakes, either.

Bake a meatloaf or roast a chicken. Steam some fresh green beans or broccoli. Nuke a sweet potato. Put the can opener away and share a freshly prepared meal with your pet. It's good for both of you.

If you cannot do this every day, do it whenever you can. Any freshly prepared meats, grains or vegetables added to your dog's diet will contribute a new level of nutrients that your pet may not be receiving from commercial food.

A big question remains: Is it worth the extra planning and the extra effort to feed your dog natural foods? You bet it is. Patou is 14 years old now and still chugging along. He has lived the equivalent of two lifetimes with us.

As most dogs age they lose muscle tone, and as their flesh has less elasticity they develop a gaunt look about their heads. Patou still has a full fleshy look, giving him the appearance of a much younger dog. His eyes are a bit cloudy, he has some minor growths and I know some days his old bones ache. But overall, he remains in excellent health. Patou is the oldest male Great Pyrenees by six years that we have ever had. I am certain that the nine years of eating an extensive variety of home prepared foods have slowed down the aging process for him.

While I know we cannot permanently halt the process of aging, many of the nutritious gifts of Mother Nature (both known and, currently, unknown) can certainly put the brakes on it.

The Vegetable Connection

Shortly after I started feeding natural foods to our dogs, a neighbor passed a large bag of just picked green beans over the fence to us. I began to tip and tail them for dinner while sitting in our backyard. Patou came over to watch the process. He hit me with his nose, so I gave him a green bean. He loved it. I gave him more. He was delighted. So I gave him more. In fact, I gave him too many. He got sick.

But he became a green bean aficionado. Green beans became the snack of choice. As he got older and more savvy, he would inspect incoming grocery bags for green beans. (I swear he could figure out what was planned for the week's menu from his forays into the bags.) If they were in there, he would annoy me until I would rinse off a few and give them to him. He ate them like candy. If you have ever eaten freshly picked green beans, you probably tasted the sugar in them. They would certainly taste like candy to a discriminating canine. So raw green beans became part of his regular diet.

And it was in this way that Patou's diet evolved. It was on his initiative that we began to feed fresh vegetables with his meals. Patou was responding to the natural cravings of his body. I was responding to Patou by making these foods available. I prepared fresh vegetables for Ed and me, so it took almost no effort to purchase a larger quantity and prepare enough for all of us.

Free Radicals

I thought I was just catering to Patou's discriminating palate, until a few years ago I learned that, in reality, I was doing something very good for Patou's body.

In 1994, a panel of experts at the Western Veterinary Conference in Las Vegas referred to antioxidants as the "missing link" in commercial dog food. They had determined that vitamins E, C and beta-carotene work the same way in canines as they do in humans. They defuse toxic molecules known as "free radicals." Free radicals are formed as a result of normal metabolism in the cells, as well as by exposure to environmental pollutants. If left unchecked, they can damage DNA, corrode cell membranes and kill cells outright.

Free radicals have been implicated in some cancers, heart and lung disease, and cataracts. Their cumulative effects may be responsible for accelerating the aging process and altering the body's immune system.

Both vitamins E and C have a high safety level, and should be routinely given as a supplement along with vitamin A. The antioxidants are available in great abundance in many vegetables, particularly the bright orange and dark green ones. By including one of these vegetables in your dog's daily ration, you are buying a small insurance policy for good health. Patou's instincts were excellent.

All leafy green vegetables are a wonderful source of antioxidants and fiber. Some also contain calcium, potassium, manganese, iron, phosphorous or niacin. Many cruciferous vegetables such as broccoli, Brussels sprouts and cauliflower contain compounds that stimulate the body's natural defenses to neutralize carcinogens, which are cancer causing compounds. And this is only a short recap of the positive benefits of some of the vegetables readily available for you and your dog. It just takes a little time and a little preparation.

If you follow the Scatter-Shot Theory of good nutrition, you do not need to know which vegetables contain what nutrients, because you should treat the world of vegetables like a self-serve salad bar. Take a little of each, some raw, some cooked. Your dog, like you, may not enjoy each and every vegetable, but there are so many to choose from, you will find some that your pet likes. Just make certain each week you provide some greens, some cruciferous vegetables like broccoli and cabbage, and anti-oxidant rich vegetables like sweet potatoes and carrots.

Offer variety, keep carbohydrates, proteins and vegetables in balance, and supply and use everything in moderation.

Natural Foods

When you make the decision to start your dog on natural food, you will see that it is more preparation than anything else. Your success begins with your mindset in the grocery store. You have to think in terms of purchasing larger quantities and preparing bigger portions. Remember that *you want leftovers.*

Also, think in terms of expanding the food options for your entire family. Try at the very least to add one new vegetable, herb or spice each month. You can begin to experiment, and at each new level you will expand the variety of foods and groups of food that you and your pet will eat.

Start simply and start slowly. But start.

Preparing for the Switch

In switching to natural foods, give your dog's body adequate time to adjust to the change in diet. Allow approximately two weeks to complete the switch.

Keep careful track of what you are feeding and how your dog reacts to it. If there is a negative reaction to a food or a group of foods, temporarily eliminate that food from the diet.

You will find foods that your dog will not eat now and never will eat. And there may be some foods that cause illness or an allergic reaction. You will be able to find suitable substitutes for any specific food that causes a problem.

Any food that causes a negative reaction in your dog should be eliminated from the diet. If, for example, your dog has an allergic reaction to corn, simply eliminate corn and all corn products from the diet. Don't feed your dog corn meal, corn flakes, corn bread, polenta or grits. You will not be blind-sided by a mysterious ingredient incorporated into the food (as can

PRIMARY VITAMINS AND MINERALS AND THEIR COMMON NATURAL FOOD SOURCES

Vitamin A Beta-carotene	fish liver oil, watercress, kale, garlic, dandelion greens, carrots, beets, spinach, Swiss chard, sweet potatoes, yellow squash, broccoli, mustard and turnip greens
Vitamin D	sunshine, egg yolks, butter, milk, halibut, cod liver oil, salmon, tuna, oatmeal, sweet potatoes, vegetable oils
Vitamin C plus bioflavonoids	onions, collards, broccoli, turnip, beet and mustard greens, kale, sweet peppers (especially red), turnips, asparagus, spinach, Brussels sprouts, Swiss chard, green peas, tomatoes
Vitamin F	salmon, wheat germ, olive and other vegetable oils, spinach, parsley, all dark leafy green vegetables
Vitamin K	egg yolks, blackstrap molasses, oatmeal, wheat and rye flour, liver, cabbage, cauliflower, corn, kale, green peas, root vegetables, kelp, all leafy green vegetables
B Vitamins	wheat germ, brewer's yeast, brown rice, nuts, seeds, oats, whole grains, lentils, lima and kidney beans, egg yolks, buckwheat flour, green peas, asparagus, Brussels sprouts
Vitamin E	wheat germ, cold pressed oils, dry beans, brown rice, nuts, milk, eggs, cornmeal, oatmeal, all leafy green vegetables
Calcium	yogurt, milk and milk products, collards, asparagus, kale, tofu, brewer's yeast, oats, broccoli, kelp, all leafy green vegetables
Chloride	animal foods, table salt
Chromium	corn oil, whole grain cereals, meats, brewer's yeast, dried beans, cheese, potatoes, brown rice
Copper	kidneys, egg yolks, legumes, whole grains, soybeans, oats, nuts
Iodine	seafood (fish, shellfish and plants), table salt, onions, garlic, spinach, carrots, tomatoes, cod liver oil
Iron	meat, poultry, fish, eggs, bread and cereals (enriched with iron), potatoes, milk, blackstrap molasses, beets, asparagus, leafy green vegetables
Magnesium	milk and dairy, meat, fish and seafood, peanuts, blackstrap molasses, kelp, soybeans, wheat germ, oatmeal, cornmeal, rice, brewer's yeast, fresh green vegetables
Manganese	whole grain cereals, egg yolks, nuts and seeds, spinach and other leafy green vegetables

Phosphorus	milk and dairy products, meat, fish, garlic, asparagus, brewer's yeast, whole grains
Potassium	bananas, whole grains, mint leaves, potatoes, dairy products (particularly cheese), meats, poultry, fish, legumes, nuts, garlic, brewer's yeast, yogurt, all leafy green vegetables
Selenium	bran and germ cereals, broccoli, onions, tomatoes, tuna, brewer's yeast, garlic, brown rice, chicken, turkey, fish
Zinc	meats, poultry (dark meat), fish and seafood, liver, eggs, legumes, whole grains, brewer's yeast, mushrooms, wheat germ, soybeans

happen with commercially prepared foods) because you control everything that goes into the food bowl.

Your dog is an individual and is entitled to individual tastes. Consider the country of origin of your breed of dog. Learn what kinds of foods the human population there eats and consider incorporating those foods into your dog's menu. Great Pyrenees lived in the mountains between France and Spain for 3,000 years before coming to America. Why should we be surprised that most of them love French bread?

If you have not been supplementing your dog's diet before, you may want to do so as part of this program. Ask your veterinarian or your dog's breeder for suggested amounts of vitamins C and E, cod liver oil (in capsule form), and multivitamins and minerals to add.

Consider your dog's country of origin. Learn what kinds of food the human population there eats. (Photo by Ed Boyle)

Avoid any one specific vitamin or mineral, except for those listed here. Many individual vitamins or minerals require other complementary elements in very specific ratios (for example, calcium and phosphorus) in order to be of benefit, and worse, to prevent damage. Concentrate on an abundance of good fresh natural foods, emphasize variety, and keep the carbohydrates, proteins and vegetables in balance.

Making the Switch

The following is a recommended timetable for switching your dog to natural foods. Use this as a guide only. If your dog is having a difficult time making the transition, slow it down. If your dog is enjoying the changes, as I suspect it will, do not speed up the process. Take the full two weeks to switch to natural foods. You must give the dog's digestive system time to adjust to this new diet.

Week 1

A typical canine diet consists of dry kibble and a meat-based mix, either canned or frozen. Because you may already be providing variety in the meat mix department, this becomes the easiest to change. Keep the kibble the same and each day add more real meat and decrease the commercial variety as follows:

Day 1: Kibble and $^3/_4$ meat mix with $^1/_4$ real meat

Day 2: Kibble and $^1/_2$ meat mix with $^1/_2$ real meat

Day 3: Kibble and $^1/_4$ meat mix with $^3/_4$ real meat

Day 4: Kibble and real meat

Days 5–7: Kibble and real meat, with some vegetables

Use days 5, 6 and 7 to stabilize the diet. Vary the home-prepared meats between beef, chicken and lamb. Begin to add some sweet vegetables to the meal in the form of cooked carrots or sweet potatoes.

Week 2

Slowly eliminate the kibble as follows:

Day 8: Meat, vegetables, $^3/_4$ kibble and $^1/_4$ rice

Day 9: Meat, vegetables, $^1/_2$ kibble and $^1/_2$ rice

Day 10: Meat, vegetables, $^1/_4$ kibble and $^3/_4$ rice

Days 12–14: Meat, vegetables and rice (or other carbohydrates)

Use days 12 through 14 to stabilize the diet, adding variety in the carbohydrates by using pasta, barley, grits and other grains.

Weeks 3 and 4
When all your dog's systems are stable, begin expanding the vegetable offerings. Prepare what is in season and fresh. Asparagus, carrots, green beans, wax beans, chard, eggplant, peas, potatoes and all winter and summer squash are good choices. Add the sweet potatoes twice a week.

The nutritional needs of your dog will change with the seasons and its levels of activity in any given period of time. To guarantee adequate food during periods of stress, be flexible with the amounts given. But try to stay with the approximate balance of 40 to 60 percent carbohydrate/grains, and 20 to 30 percent each meat and vegetables.

Establishing the Maintenance Diet

The bulk volume of the canine diet should consist of complex carbohydrates. These supply the dog with energy and, when made available with protein, facilitate tissue development. They also stress the excretory systems less than proteins, and generally have fewer pesticides and other pollutants affiliated with them.

Common carbohydrates are pasta, rice, grits and cereals. Supplement these with slices of fresh French bread or whole wheat bread. Periodically, you may want to add barley, lentils or kidney beans, as well.

A maintenance diet uses proportions of two parts carbohydrates to one part each of low-fat meat and cooked vegetables. This ratio seems to put minimum stress on the body systems while offering adequate maintenance for a house pet. If you physically divide your dog's diet into quarters, two of those quarters by volume should be carbohydrates. If you are serving four cups of food, make two cups cooked rice or pasta, one cup low-fat meat and one cup vegetables.

When you start serving natural food to your dog, you may have to adjust these ratios. You want your dog eating the meat portion (no problem) as well as the vegetables (potential problem). The carbohydrates are to round out the meal and provide your pet with that comfortable "full" (not stuffed) feeling.

As you expand your variety of meals for your dog, concentrate on providing those foods that we know are good for us, such as garlic, yogurt, sweet potatoes and cruciferous vegetables. You will not be able to provide a 100 percent balance every day, but over a period of a month you should offer enough variety in meats, carbohydrates/grains and vegetables to benefit from The Scatter-Shot Theory of good nutrition. Remember—variety, moderation and balance.

Every day your dog should get the following:

- Two parts complex carbohydrates, such as rice or pasta (rice will be a little more dense than a pasta such as elbow macaroni, so you may have to increase the amount of pasta)
- One part cooked vegetables
- One part low-fat meat

In addition, every week add the following:

- Two servings of sweet potatoes
- Three raw vegetables (for example, grated carrots, cole slaw, raw green beans or chopped greens)
- Two to three servings of dairy products (low-fat milk, yogurt or cottage cheese)

Monthly, add the following:

- Two meals of chicken or beef liver
- Four eggs

A typical meal would consist of the following, by volume:

- Two parts cooked pasta or rice
- One part low-fat meat
- One part cooked green beans
- One slice sweet potato or a quarter cup grated carrots

Think in terms of cooking these meals for your dog, then having the dog share its dinner with you; consider meals like chicken with broccoli and rice, or meatloaf with mashed potatoes and green beans. By making home prepared meals for your pet, you share in the benefits.

The following are suggested meal combinations, by volume, for your dog:

Suggestion One

- Two parts rice
- One part chicken

- One part broccoli
- Some grated carrots

Suggestion Two

- Two parts mashed potatoes
- One part meatloaf
- One part green beans
- Some coleslaw

Suggestion Three

- Two parts pasta
- One part beef stew
- One part sautéed greens (Sautéed greens are tricky because they collapse to almost nothing. A quarter or half part of these would be adequate.)

The combinations are endless and are limited only by your imagination. Concentrate on freshness and variety; balance the ingredients and practice moderation in all aspects of the diet.

In addition, supplement with vitamins C and E and cod liver oil. And if your dog's coat appears somewhat dry, add one teaspoon to one tablespoon of vegetable oil. But closely monitor your dog's weight if you choose to add the oil.

Get the Fat Out

Most dogs are no longer performing the functions for which their breed was created or originally used—pulling sleds or carts, or guarding or herding flocks of sheep or cattle, or going to ground to capture vermin.

They are much more likely to be house pets, guarding their front window or backyard from predators, or alerting their masters to company. Some just enjoy being a pet, a companion and a couch potato. And there is nothing wrong with that.

Dogs seem to know instinctively that when you pet them, your blood pressure goes down; that when you talk to them or worry about them, you change the stress vectors in your life and, in so doing, make living more pleasurable for everyone. Dogs give pleasure to their humans by just being. And this does not require a great deal of energy.

Few dogs perform the work for which they were bred. We must take this into consideration when we feed them. Ann Boles helps Kolby teach the puppy Deva how to behave as a potential therapy dog. (Photo by Jim Boles)

A sedentary animal consuming too much food will convert this excess to fat and store it for future use. If periods of fasting or famine are too few or non-existent, the dog keeps this fat in storage. If you increase your dog's exercise and reduce the amount of food consumed, the body will begin to tap into this stored fat.

Fat occurs naturally in meat and vegetables. What little fat is needed for everyday consumption will be available in abundance in a natural diet. What you will want to do, especially if you have an older or inactive dog, is monitor the fat levels and keep them low.

Fat quickly satisfies an appetite. A high-fat diet will mean your pet will fill up on fat to the exclusion of other good foods that should be consumed— foods like sweet potatoes, broccoli and green beans.

If hungry and given a choice between a bacon double cheeseburger and a stalk of broccoli, both the owner and the pet will choose the burger. Once in awhile this is okay, but for the daily diet keep the fat content low. This will make the occasional cheeseburger a real treat.

Again, we are aiming for a balance, and no one will be able to provide an exact formula and percentages for your dog. But neither do you need to see the results tomorrow. Your pet is going to be with you for a long time. Use this time to determine exactly the right amount of food to give your dog at any time. This amount will change with the seasons, with the age of the dog and with your patterns of life. You will learn to gauge weight and what is right for your dog, and through trial and error will help your pet maintain its ideal weight.

If your dog is too heavy, try the following feeding techniques:

- Divide the food into two meals: breakfast and dinner. The stress of being hungry all day may contribute to your pet's over-eating. Even if you have limited time, give your pet a bowl of cereal or a toasted bagel for breakfast.

- If you use whole milk, switch to skim.

- Trim all visible fat from meat and skim the fat from all gravies.

- Use the leaner cuts of beef such as bottom, top and eye round roasts for stews instead of the more fatty cuts of beef like chuck.

- Avoid hamburger unless you can pour off all of the fat before continuing with your recipe. If you are cooking it in a recipe where you cannot pour off the fat, use only the leanest chopped beef you can buy or try substituting ground turkey.

- White chicken or turkey meat is lower in fat and calories than dark meat, but do not feed the skin. Fresh ham has all of the fat along the outside, where it is easy to trim off.

- Use Teflon frying pans so you can use less fat for cooking.

- Braise, broil, poach or roast.

- Keep frying to a minimum.

- Don't allow your pet to snack on cheese, buttered popcorn or potato chips. Try unsalted pretzels, bagels or matzos for the munchies.

If your dog is too thin, try the following:

- Increase the amount you feed your dog by 25 percent. Assume you have simply been underfeeding your dog. Increase the food available and, hopefully, over a few months your dog will be back up to a healthy weight.

- If your dog refuses to eat more food, try adding a small amount of fat to the food in the form of vegetable oil. If your dog will eat this, the fat will increase the calories consumed in any given meal. If your dog eats less because of the fat, discontinue the oil.

⊂ If your dog eats more and does not put on weight but simply increases stool sizes, you may need to add digestive enzymes to the food to allow the nutrients available to be absorbed. And of course, check for internal parasites.

Some pets might just be on the thin side. Some related individuals within the same breeding program will remain thin, while others stay at *their* ideal, somewhat heavier, weight. And if these individuals are otherwise healthy, what should you do? Kiss them on the snout and pat them on the head. They are fine. We are the ones with the problem.

The Proper Maintenance Diet for Your Dog

When we had our kennel, and even today with our dog, we prefer that they eat their fill. To do this, we intentionally overfeed the dog. This allows the dog the opportunity to determine the right amount of food it needs to maintain a proper body weight. (There *are* some dogs who will eat until they burst. Obviously, this is something you will have to learn about your dog. If you truly are the owner of a glutton, this method will not work for you.) For all the Pyrs who have lived with us, we never had an overweight dog, and we always preferred our dogs on the lean side.

The weather and the exercise program directly influence the proper amount for any dog to consume on any given day. As variable as these factors might be, that is how variable the dog's appetite might be. So don't make a big deal over some uneaten food. Dogs don't want to know about the starving canines in other parts of the world.

With this in mind, I like to overfeed Patou. I like him to leave some food. He will usually eat all of the meat and vegetables, then eat the rice or pasta until he is full. This always takes less than 20 minutes. Within 20 minutes of starting to eat, he will either have eaten everything or eaten all he will. Any uneaten food is removed and saved or discarded.

If you have a dog that constantly eats everything offered, you may have to show restraint in how much you serve. We are all happy to have our meals appreciated, but if you have a couch potato eating like a working dog you will end up with an overstuffed animal. If your dog is constantly hungry and is gaining weight (and the veterinarian confirms that the dog is otherwise healthy), decrease the amount of grains/carbohydrates and meat by 25 percent and make up the difference in volume with vegetables.

Offer some raw vegetables with crunch, like iceberg lettuce and raw green beans.

Gauging the Proper Weight of Your Dog

In attempting to determine the proper weight for your dog, get used to feeling for the ribs. Ed and I call this the "hand-eye" method of grading proper weight.

Learn to gauge the proper weight of your dog. (Photo by Ed Boyle)

If your dog is one of the sighthounds like the Greyhound or Saluki, you want to see the ribs of the dog. For the majority of other breeds, this is too thin. To complicate matters, many dogs have dense coats that make the ribs invisible, regardless of how thin the dogs are.

So for this, you have to use your imagination and your hands. Visualize a skeleton. Run your hand over your dog's ribs. If you can visualize every rib under the coat, your dog is too thin. If you can't find any ribs at all, your dog is too heavy. This method gives lots of latitude.

When you first begin working out the right amount of food to feed, make a point of using this method at least once a week as a part of the grooming ritual. It will, over time, become so automatic that you will not even realize you are doing it. The simple act of petting your dog will give you immediate feedback about its weight.

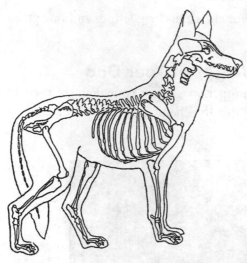

To gauge the proper weight of your dog, visualize the canine skeleton.

If you are uncertain about the proper weight for your dog, speak to your veterinarian about your dog's current weight in relationship to your dog's breed (or predominant type, in the case of a mixed breed).

Remember that growth spurts, levels of activity and seasonal changes will affect the amounts of food consumed. Your constant monitoring of the flesh covering the ribs will give you feedback on the need to increase or decrease portions. This constant monitoring will also alert you to any medical problems that involve loss of weight.

How Frequently Should You Feed Your Dog?

Puppies should be fed at least three times per day until they get to the point where they choose not to eat one meal. Then you can drop them back to two meals per day.

Any dog undergoing stress should be fed more frequently, but perhaps smaller meals each time, as your veterinarian advises. Feed pregnant and lactating bitches at least three meals a day. Working or performance dogs should be fed twice a day.

Years ago I fed my adults only a "cookie" in the morning and then a large meal in the evening. Only having one dog now, I take the time to feed him twice a day. And he looks forward to his breakfast.

To make it simple, I usually prepare a large dinner, then divide it. I feed a larger part of the meal in the evening and the remaining part the next morning. I put his breakfast in a ceramic pasta bowl or Pyrex pie plate. This makes reheating in the microwave easy, and the bowls go into the dishwasher later. Stainless steel bowls, while most practical, cannot go into the microwave. And avoid using plastic bowls.

Heating the food in the microwave takes seconds to do and makes such a big difference. Most foods smell and taste better warm for humans and, I assume, for a dog whose nose is keener than ours.

If you stir the food with a spoon, make certain you test the temperature with your finger. Certain foods get hotter than others in a microwave, and you don't want to burn your dog.

Apply simple hygienic practices. Twenty minutes after you serve the meal, pick up the bowl. Save or trash anything that is left over (your decision), and wash out the bowl with non-harsh detergent or put it in the dishwasher.

You don't want to feed good quality natural food then ruin it by putting it in a food encrusted bowl, or one that reeks of detergent.

You Can—But Should You?

Whenever other dog owners learn that I feed my dog natural foods, they always have one question: What do you feed? I always answer this with another question: If you were going to make a healthy meal for yourself, what would you prepare? The answer is almost uniformly: chicken, rice and broccoli.

We know what is good for us. We may not always choose to eat properly, but most of us know how to do so. And the same applies to feeding our dogs. We and our dogs are very much alike. Our canine counterparts travel a little closer to the ground than we do. Give them the opportunity to get closer to those things that are grown, not manufactured.

There are untold riches in the world of food. Freshly grown and home-prepared foods offer an abundance of benefits. Share this wealth, and thereby the health and long life with those you love, both canine and human.

PART II

Recipes

Chapter 3

Appetizers

HUMMUS WITH RED PEPPERS

We rarely eat appetizers, except if we have company or dinner has been delayed. But we are all guilty of raiding the refrigerator for a late night snack, on occasion. As we "veg out" after a long day, we all nibble on these.

2 16-oz. cans garbanzo beans,
    drained and rinsed
1/3 cup tahini
Juice of one lemon
2 cloves garlic, minced

1/2 tsp. salt
Black pepper to taste
1/2 cup roasted red pepper (yours or
    jarred), diced small

Put all of the ingredients except the red pepper in the bowl of a food processor and pulse on and off until pureed. Remove hummus from the processor and stir in the roasted red peppers. Refrigerate at least 2 hours to let flavors develop. Can be made up to 3 days ahead.

Bring to room temperature before serving. Serve as a dip for fresh raw vegetables and slices of pita bread.

Makes 8 appetizer servings

TOASTED FRENCH BREAD

Slice French bread into diagonal slices. Place under the broiler or on an open grill until the edges toast and the bread turns a golden brown. (This happens quickly, so watch carefully.)

Serve with the roasted garlic heads. (Some added butter is optional.)

Makes 6 appetizer servings

ROASTED GARLIC

I love garlic, and this is a particularly wonderful way to prepare it. Garlic is one of those good-for-you foods, as is the olive oil. And if no one in your household likes this dish, I guarantee your dog will love it.

6 heads garlic
1 T. olive oil

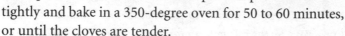

Cut off the tops (the pointed ends) of the garlic heads. Take off some, but not all, of the papery skin. Place in heavy duty tin foil and sprinkle the oil over the tops. Wrap tightly and bake in a 350-degree oven for 50 to 60 minutes, or until the cloves are tender.

Squeeze garlic out of the skins and spread onto toasted French bread.

BOILED SHRIMP

If I have one major weakness in cooking seafood, it is overcooking it. My boiled shrimp used to have the texture of a rubber tire until a friend enlightened me. This is a "don't leave the kitchen for a second" recipe.

1 lb. large shrimp, shells on

Place the shrimp in a colander and rinse with cold running water for about 2 minutes. Place the rinsed shrimp into a tall pot with enough water to cover the shrimp by 1 1/2 to 2 inches.

Place the pot over high heat and heat to a boil, gently stirring occasionally. (You just want the shrimp to circulate gently in the pot.) The minute the shrimp come to a full boil, stir them once then remove them from the heat. Pour the contents of the pot into the colander and rinse under cold running water until the shrimp are cooled. Refrigerate until serving.

(If you have a small dog, you may need to peel the shrimp before serving it. Watch your dog closely to see how it handles shrimp shells.)

Makes 6 generous servings

Chapter 4

Soups

During the winter, most Saturday mornings I make a pot of soup, which is lunch for all of us on Saturday and my lunch for the rest of the week. I usually make the broth one night during the week, let it cool to skim the fat off, and then I finish making the soup on Saturday morning.

I will make a pot of soup and use the microwave oven in the office to heat up a bowl for lunch. With a slice of hearty peasant bread, it is a nutritious, tasty and easy lunch.

My Great Pyrenees Patou watches me in the kitchen, but does not stay underfoot. He has had his share of stepped on paws and pans bouncing off the dish rack. But as the soup cooking progresses, he will invariably wander in to check the status. And after we have eaten, he will make it known whether or not this soup interests him. If it does, we cool some down for him.

Because I don't know how to make a small pot of soup, I am happy to share with Patou. He is happy to have it warmed for breakfast, and sometimes poured over leftover rice or pasta, especially on those bitter winter mornings after guarding his snow-covered backyard.

CHICKEN SOUP

Prepare the stock:

2 small chickens or the meaty remains
    of a large roaster
Cold water to cover

Bring the water to a simmer and skim whatever scum rises to the surface. Let the chicken simmer slowly for 1 hour. Allow the chicken to cool in the pot until cool enough to handle. Pick all the meat off the skin and bones. Refrigerate the meat. Return skin and bones to the pot with the liquid. Where possible, crack the bones. Bring back to a simmer.

Add:

1 large onion stuck with 4 cloves
2 carrots
1 rib celery

8 peppercorns
1 chicken bouillon cube
Parsley stems

Cover and simmer for 2 hours longer. Strain solids from the pot. Refrigerate liquid overnight, and before continuing remove the congealed fat from the top of the soup. (If you have a fat separator you can use that, then simply continue with the recipe.)

Prepare the soup:

Prepared chicken broth
1 large onion, sliced
2 T. vegetable oil
1 bay leaf, crushed
3 large carrots, sliced

6 stalks celery, sliced
1 cube chicken bouillon
10–15 strands linguini, broken into
    2-inch pieces

In a large Dutch oven, bring the prepared stock to a boil.

In a separate frying pan, sauté the onion in the vegetable oil until translucent. Add the crushed bay leaf, carrots and celery and continue sautéing until carrots begin to soften (about 15 minutes), stirring occasionally. Pour contents of the frying pan into the broth.

Simmer for another half hour. During the last 20 minutes, add the linguini and cook until tender. Just before serving, add some of the boned chicken meat and heat through. Serve hot to humans. Let it cool to tepid for your dog.

Makes 8 generous servings

Bean Soups

I used to wait until I had a smoked ham before making bean soup. Then I moved on to smoked hocks. Now I use smoked turkey legs. They provide the same smoky flavor, more meat and less fat. I usually don't even bother to cool the stock to congeal the fat, since there's almost none, but proceed through the entire recipe in one shot.

BEAN WITH BACON SOUP

1 lb. dried great northern beans
1 turkey thigh or drumstick, smoked
1/4 lb. bacon
2 T. vegetable oil
3 medium onions, chopped
3 cloves garlic, chopped

3 ribs celery, chopped
3 carrots, peeled and diced
3 T. chopped parsley
Salt and pepper to taste
1 T. vinegar

Wash beans and pick over for any foreign material. Place in a large Dutch oven or soup pot and cover with water. Bring to a boil, cover and let stand for 1 hour. Drain the beans and return to the soup pot with 2 quarts of water and the turkey leg. Cover, bring to a boil, then reduce heat to allow the beans to simmer.

In another skillet, cook the bacon. Remove the bacon and drain the fat. Heat the vegetable oil (to be authentic you should use 2 T. of bacon fat; do what you think best) in the skillet and add the onions, celery, carrots and garlic. Cook until the onions are transparent. Add to the beans. Cover and cook for 2 hours. Then remove the turkey leg and allow it to cool until the meat can be removed. Chop the meat and put it back in the soup.

With a slotted spoon, remove 1 1/2 cups beans and puree in a blender or food processor. Return to the pot with the turkey meat. Add parsley and simmer another 30 minutes. Season with salt, pepper and vinegar.

Makes 10 servings

LENTIL SOUP

I love a hearty soup, and this lentil soup fits the bill. I don't like the color of the lentils, so I add the canned tomatoes. This also gives it more of a soup consistency.

1 lb. lentils, washed and sorted
1 turkey drumstick, smoked
2–3 quarts cold water
1 T. vegetable oil
1 medium onion, diced
3 stalks celery, chopped in
   $1/2$-inch pieces

3 carrots, chopped in
   $1/2$-inch pieces
3 cloves garlic, minced
2 bay leaves, crushed
1 28-oz. can plum tomatoes,
   undrained

Put the turkey drumstick in water and bring to a boil. Reduce heat, cover and simmer for $1^1/2$ hours.

In a separate frying pan, sauté the onion, celery and carrots until the onion turns clear. Add garlic and bay leaves and sauté until you begin to smell their aroma. Add this to the simmering stock. Add lentils to the stock and continue simmering for another hour.

Remove the drumstick and cool. Add the can of plum tomatoes, either breaking the tomatoes up with your hands or chopping them with a knife.

Simmer the soup uncovered for another half hour.

When the turkey is cool enough to handle, remove the meat and chop into small pieces. Return this to the soup to heat through. Serve soup piping hot to humans, sprinkled generously with Parmesan cheese and with a side of hot pepper sauce.

Cool slightly for your pet and forget the hot sauce.

Makes 10 servings

🦴 🦴 🦴 🦴 🦴

PASTA & BEAN SOUP

I developed this soup because I had chicken stock in the refrigerator and couldn't face another pot of chicken noodle soup. I loved this soup in restaurants, but never found a hearty enough recipe for it. Again, this is a lunch all by itself.

$1/2$ lb. dried great northern beans,
   washed and picked over
2 quarts water
2 quarts chicken broth
1 T. vegetable oil
1 medium onion, diced
3 stalks celery, chopped in
   $1/2$-inch pieces

3 carrots, chopped in
   $1/2$-inch pieces
3 cloves garlic, minced
1 T. dried oregano or basil
1 16-oz. can tomatoes,
   undrained
$1/2$ cup small pasta, cooked
   and drained

Wash the beans and pick over for any foreign material. Place in a large Dutch oven or soup pot and cover with water. Bring to a boil, cover and let stand for 1 hour. Drain beans and return to soup pot with water to cover. Bring to a boil. Reduce heat and simmer for 1¹/₂ hours or until beans are tender.

Bring chicken stock to a simmer.

In a separate frying pan, sauté the onion, celery and carrots until the onion turns clear. Add garlic and oregano or basil and sauté until you begin to smell the seasonings. Add the tomatoes, breaking them up as you add them.

Using a slotted spoon, take 1 cup of the onion-celery mixture and put in a blender or food processor. Add to this 1 cup of the cooked beans. Puree the mixture and add it to the simmering stock.

Add the rest of the sautéed vegetable mixture and the rest of the beans. Simmer for another half an hour. Add the cooked pasta and serve with grated Parmesan cheese.

Makes 6 to 8 servings

VEGETABLE BEEF SOUP

2 rounds of beef shins, about 2 lb. each with bone in
2 bay leaves
2 celery stalks, chopped
1 medium onion, diced
4 carrots, chopped

1 cup cabbage, sliced
1-lb. can Italian-style tomatoes
1 T. Worcestershire sauce
1 T. oregano or basil
1 cube beef bouillon

Cover the meat with water. Add bay leaves and bring to a simmer. Skim the scum off the surface.

Add the celery, onion, carrots and cabbage. Cover and continue simmering for 2¹/₂ to 3 hours, or until the meat is very tender.

When the meat is tender, remove from the pot and cool. When it's cool enough to handle, cut into bite-sized pieces. Return meat to the soup. Add the tomatoes, Worcestershire sauce, bouillon cube and oregano or basil. Simmer for 30 minutes more.

Adjust the seasoning, and add salt and pepper to taste.

Makes 6 servings

BEEF BARLEY SOUP

I love barley. I love the texture of it when it has simmered for a long time. It's smooth and velvety, and I find it real comfort food.

This recipe was given to me by my Aunt Cat. Her husband loved barley as much as I do, and he loved this soup. I have made this with fresh mushrooms, but have also, on occasion, made it with leftover sautéed mushrooms, and frequently with canned beef stock.

Prepare beef stock:

1 lb. beef stew meat, cubed
2 quarts cold water

Cook beef in water until tender, about 2¹/₂ hours. Remove meat from stock and refrigerate stock and beef separately. When stock is chilled, remove fat from the surface and continue with the recipe (or decant stock in a fat skimmer, and continue).

Make soup:

2 T. vegetable oil
1 onion, diced
3 carrots, cubed
1 stalk celery, diced

2 potatoes, peeled and diced
2 T. parsley, chopped
¹/₂ lb. mushrooms, sliced
¹/₂ cup barley

In a large pot, sauté the onion, carrots and celery in the oil until golden. Add the remaining ingredients and sauté lightly. Add the beef broth. Bring to a simmer, cover and cook for 1¹/₂ hours. Add the reserved beef, uncover and simmer for 20 more minutes.

Taste, and add salt and pepper if desired.

Makes 8 servings

Chapter 5

Poultry

Tips on Buying and Handling Poultry

Chicken comes in many different forms: whole, parts, boneless, boned, ground or pre-prepared and ready to cook. Choose the right form for the right recipe. Believe it or not, most dogs really appreciate the difference. Different flavors and textures can stimulate a dog's appetite, even if the type of meat is the same.

When dealing with any raw meat, including poultry, don't cross contaminate. Don't let any raw meat or its juices come in contact with cooked foods or foods that will not be cooked. If there are illness-causing bacteria in the meat, we do not want them in contact with foods that will not be heated to a temperature high enough to destroy them.

Chickens can carry salmonella, a bacteria that can cause severe illness and sometimes death. Salmonella is killed by heat, and because of this all poultry should be cooked thoroughly and to a temperature high enough to destroy this organism. Treat all chicken as if it were contaminated. Wash your hands and any surface that has come into contact with the poultry with hot, soapy water. And cook all chicken until the meat is opaque and the juices run clear.

I also Kosher my chicken. My mother always treated whole chickens and turkeys this way, and a Jewish friend told me that it was done to take the blood out of the fowl. I think my mother did it as a way of further cleaning the chicken. I do it because I much prefer chicken after it has been treated this way. It is sweeter and more delicate.

To Kosher a Chicken

Take a pot large enough to hold the bird (I have to do my turkeys in the kitchen sink). Take the poultry out of the wrapper and remove the neck and the other organs. Rinse the cavity with cold running tap water and drain. Pull out any unwanted leftovers from the inside and remove any large chunks of fat.

Put the poultry in the pot or the kitchen sink. Place at least 1 tablespoon (for a chicken) and up to 3 tablespoons (for a turkey) of Kosher salt in the cavity. Fill the pot or sink with enough water to cover and fill the entire cavity of the bird.

Let the poultry soak for at least 15 minutes and up to one hour. (I prefer the longer times.) Then remove the bird, rinse and pat dry. Proceed with any recipes for whole chicken or turkey.

Wash everything well with hot, soapy water.

COMPANY ROASTED CHICKEN

Most Sunday dinners of my childhood consisted of a roasted capon stuffed with my mother's sausage stuffing. I no longer stuff the chicken because of the time factor. A simple roasted chicken makes an easy Sunday meal with leftovers for the week.

This recipe also works for turkey, but bake it for 15 to 20 minutes per pound, or until the juices run clear.

1 chicken	3 cloves garlic, crushed
1 lemon	1/2 tsp. whole dried rosemary
1 onion, peeled and quartered	Garlic salt

Kosher the chicken, as described. Place the wings behind the back to form a self-contained rack. Cut the lemon in half and squeeze the juice over the entire chicken.

Put the lemon rinds in the cavity with the garlic and onion. With butcher's twine or white string, tie the two legs together. (This will allow for a nicer presentation, but the new thinking is that because dark meat takes longer to cook than white, the legs should not be tied together because it slows the cooking.)

Put the rosemary in the palm of your hand and crush it into smaller pieces. Sprinkle this and some garlic salt onto the chicken breasts and legs. Place the chicken breast up in the roasting pan and add enough chicken stock to come about 1/2 inch up the side of the pan. Put legs to the back of the oven and bake at 350 degrees until the juices between the thigh and body run clear when pierced with a fork. A small chicken (3 1/2 to 4 lb.) will take 1 1/2 hours. For larger chickens, follow the roasting chart on the wrapper.

Makes 4 servings

BARBECUED CHICKEN

Some dogs may not like barbecue sauce, and others usually prefer it in its natural state and not jazzed up, as I would do it for human consumption.

My favorite barbecue sauce is no longer available. So I take almost any kind of barbecue sauce and spike it with additional brown sugar, dry mustard, liquid smoke (sometimes) and hot pepper sauce, and create something that I do like.

Place cut up chicken pieces on a foil-lined baking sheet large enough so that the pieces will not touch. Do not leave these pieces unattended for your dogs to sample before they are cooked! Bake at 350 degrees for 1 hour. Five minutes before the pieces are done, remove from the oven and coat generously with barbecue sauce. Return to the oven for 5 more minutes.

Servings vary based on the type and quantity of pieces chosen

Boneless Chicken Breasts

I love these chicken breasts, and when they are on sale I pop a few packages in the freezer for fast meals. If the packages are very large, I will sometimes freeze individual cutlets in plastic wrap and pull out only as much as I need for a meal. They defrost in no time when packaged this way.

CHICKEN FRANCAISE

1 lb. boneless and skinless
   chicken breasts
1 cup flour
4 eggs
1 tsp. parsley
1 tsp. Parmesan cheese
1/2 tsp. garlic powder

Salt and pepper
Oil for frying
1/2 cup dry sherry
1 cup chicken broth
2 T. butter
2 lemons
Parsley to garnish

Heat oil in the bottom of a heavy pan over medium heat.

Pull filets from the bone or slice the thick part of the breast open to flatten. Pound cutlets until thin. Dredge cutlets in flour.

Mix the eggs, parsley, cheese and garlic powder in a flat pan. Dip dredged chicken breasts into the egg mixture and place in the preheated frying pan. Brown well over medium heat, then turn and brown on other side.

In a separate skillet, heat sherry, chicken broth, and butter to the boiling point. Place browned cutlets in the sherry mixture. Squeeze the juice of 2 lemons over the cutlets. Simmer for 10 minutes, then turn heat to low. This dish will keep on low for almost 1 hour.

Sprinkle with parsley and serve.

Makes 4 servings

CHICKEN PARMESAN

4 boneless chicken breast halves
Flour for dusting
2 large eggs
2 T. milk
1½ cups seasoned bread crumbs
Vegetable oil for frying

2 cups marinara sauce, divided use
4 oz. mozzarella cheese, shredded or
    cut in tiny cubes
1 lb. pasta
Parmesan cheese

Prepare the pasta according to package directions. Meanwhile, prepare boneless chicken breasts by removing the thick fillets and pounding them to about ¼ inch thick. Dust all of the chicken pieces with flour to cover lightly.

Mix together the eggs and milk. Dip prepared chicken into this mixture. Place into the seasoned bread crumbs and gently press the crumbs into the chicken. Pour enough oil in a non-stick frying pan to just cover the bottom. Heat over medium high heat. Place the coated breasts into the hot oil. Fry gently until browned nicely on both sides (about 4 minutes per side—check to make certain they are cooked through by cutting into the center of the thickest part). Remove to drain briefly on paper toweling.

Preheat the broiler. Place cooked chicken on a foil-lined broiler tray. Cover the chicken with part of the marinara sauce and top with the shredded mozzarella cheese. Broil 8 inches from heat until the cheese melts (watch carefully).

Drain the prepared pasta and mix with the remainder of the marinara sauce. Place one chicken breast portion and some pasta on a plate. Cover it all with freshly grated Parmesan cheese.

Makes 4 servings

CHINESE CHICKEN IN TOMATO GINGER SAUCE

4 T. peanut oil, divided use
3 boneless, skinless chicken breasts,
   cut into ½-inch cubes (about
   2 cups)
1 egg white
2 T. cornstarch

1 bunch scallions, chopped
   into pea-sized pieces
   (including green tops)
2 tsp. fresh ginger root, minced
2 cups broccoli

Sauce Mixture:

1 T. soy sauce
4 T. white sugar
2 T. white vinegar

3 T. tomato ketchup
3 T. dry sherry

Microwave the broccoli on high for 3 minutes, then cool it rapidly under cold running water (or blanch by dropping into boiling water for 2 minutes and then rinsing under cold water).

Mix together the chicken, egg white and cornstarch. Allow to marinate while you prepare the other mixtures.

Cut and mix together the scallions and ginger.

Mix together the soy sauce, sugar, vinegar, ketchup and sherry.

Heat 3 T. oil over high heat in a non-stick frying pan. Put the chicken mixture in the frying pan. (There should only be one layer of the chicken. If the frying pan is not large enough, divide the mixture into two batches.)

Allow the chicken to cook untouched about 3 minutes or until the chicken pieces are golden brown on one side. Turn the pieces over and break up any pieces that are stuck together. Fry this side until golden and the chicken pieces are cooked through (check by cutting one in half). Remove chicken.

Heat 1 T. oil over high heat in the same pan. Add scallions and ginger, and cook until lightly golden.

Return the chicken to the pan and add the sauce mixture. Stir gently to distribute the sauce. Stir in the pre-cooked broccoli and turn off the heat. Cover the pan and let rest for 2 minutes while the broccoli heats through.

Serve with rice.

Makes 4 servings

🦴 🦴 🦴 🦴 🦴

HOISIN CHICKEN

4 T. peanut oil, divided use
3 boneless, skinless chicken breasts,
    cut into ½-inch cubes (about
    2 cups)
1 egg white
2 T. cornstarch

1 bunch scallions, chopped
    into pea-sized pieces
    (including the green tops)
2 tsp. fresh ginger root, minced
2 cups broccoli

Sauce Mixture:

¼ cup low sodium
    soy sauce
¼ cup dry sherry
¼ cup packed brown sugar

¼ cup chicken broth
3 T. Hoisin sauce
Hot chili oil to taste

Microwave broccoli on high for 3 minutes, then cool rapidly under cold running water or blanch conventionally (as described in the previous recipe). In a separate bowl, mix together the chicken, egg white and cornstarch. Allow to marinate while you prepare the rest of the mixtures.

Cut and mix together the scallions and ginger.

Mix together the soy sauce, sugar, sherry, broth, Hoisin sauce and hot chili oil.

Heat 3 T. oil over high heat in a non-stick frying pan. Put the chicken mixture in the frying pan. (There should only be one layer of the chicken. If the frying pan is not large enough, divide the mixture into two batches.)

Allow the chicken to cook untouched about 3 minutes or until the chicken pieces are golden brown on one side. Turn pieces over and break up any pieces that are stuck together. Fry this side until golden and the chicken pieces are cooked through (check by cutting one in half). Remove chicken.

Heat 1 T. oil over high heat in the same pan. Add the scallions and ginger, and cook until lightly golden. Return the chicken to the pan and add the sauce mixture. Stir gently to distribute the sauce. Stir in the pre-cooked broccoli and turn off the heat. Cover the pan and let rest for 2 minutes while the broccoli heats through.

Serve with rice.

Makes 4 servings

Chapter 6

Meat Dishes

Beef

ROAST BEEF

My mother used to make this roast beef when I was growing up. I tried making her recipe a few times years ago, and it came out overdone and tough. The mistake I made was that I allowed it to continue cooking after it came out of the oven by cooking it in a high enamel or cast iron pot and putting the lid on to let it rest. This roast has to be cooked straight from the refrigerator in a low pan and just gently draped with tin foil to let it rest. Eye rounds are always the same approximate diameter. The larger ones are just longer. So one hour is right regardless of the weight.

1 eye round roast	Garlic salt
1 medium onion, peeled	Freshly ground black pepper

Preheat oven to 425 degrees.

Remove the roast from refrigerator and place it in a shallow pan (I spray it with vegetable oil). Add the peeled onion. Pour in enough water to come 1/2 inch up the side of the pan. Sprinkle the roast and the onion with garlic salt and freshly ground black pepper.

Roast 1 hour.

Remove from the oven and lightly drape a piece of tin foil over the top. Let the roast rest for 10 minutes. Slice very thin.

Leftovers make great sandwiches! Slice very thin and pile onto a roll with thinly sliced fresh tomatoes and raw sweet onions. Microwave on high for about 30 seconds to warm.

Number of servings varies with the weight of the roast

GERMAN POT ROAST

I've done the marinating and the waiting and the other time-consuming pot roast variations. This is my mother's recipe, one of the easiest to make and one of the tastiest. Serve it with red cabbage and mashed potatoes, or with potato pancakes for a truly German feast.

3 T. vegetable oil
1 clove garlic, minced
1/2 cup onions, coarsely chopped
3–4 lb. rump roast
3 cups boiling water
1/4 cup vinegar
1 small carrot

8 whole peppercorns
1 bay leaf, broken in half
2 cloves
Dash of ground allspice
2 tsp. salt
1/4 tsp. black pepper
Flour to thicken gravy

In a Dutch oven, sauté the garlic and onions in the oil until well browned. Remove and save. Brown the beef well on all sides in the remaining oil.

After the meat has browned, return the garlic and onions to the pot and add all of the remaining ingredients except the flour. Bring to a boil, lower heat and simmer, covered, for about 3 hours. Remove meat from the pot and strain the liquid. Thicken the gravy with 2 T. flour or more, if needed.

This is actually better made one day ahead. The meat will slice easier and you can remove the fat from the liquid before making the gravy.

Makes 8 to 10 servings

PERFECTLY GRILLED STEAK

There are two parts to a wonderfully done steak.

Part 1: Choose your meat carefully. Because these steaks go unadorned, they must be able to stand on their own. Ed loves filet mignon. We buy the butt half and cut it up ourselves. We control the size of the steaks and the dog gets the parts that cannot be cut into pieces of steak. (Of course my dog gets filet mignon. If I let the butcher cut it, these parts would wind up on the floor or somewhere else.)

Part 2: Choose your method of preparation carefully. If I am preparing it, I will use the broiler. A 3/4-inch steak will get 7 minutes on one side, then

5 minutes on the other. I let it rest, lightly covered with foil for 5 minutes before serving.

If Ed is grilling the steak, he does some massive mathematical calculations, including flame size divided by barometric pressure multiplied by wind velocity. Or something like that. It's either magical or mathematical, but it always comes out medium rare, just the way I like it.

LONDON BROIL

I use a large, 1-inch thick, 2-1/2 to 3-lb. top round cut for the London broil. Marinating overnight and cooking the meat rare will produce a flavorful, fairly tender meat with lots of leftovers for stir fry.

2–3 lb. top round London broil	1/4 cup dry sherry
1/4 cup reduced sodium soy sauce	Sliced fresh ginger root (optional)

Put meat in a zipper-seal plastic bag. Mix the soy sauce and sherry together and add to the bag (with the ginger, if you are using it). Seal the bag, removing as much air as possible. Place the bag in a nonreactive container that can hold it flat (I use a 7×11-inch Pyrex baking dish).

Let the meat marinate overnight in the refrigerator at least 12 hours, but not longer than 36. Turn over occasionally. One hour before serving, remove meat from the bag. Place meat and marinade in the pan that held the bag. Using a super sharp knife, score both sides of the meat into a 3/4-inch diamond pattern to a depth of about 1/4 inch.

Let the meat marinate for 30 minutes at room temperature, turning over a few times. In a preheated broiler, broil 7 inches from the heat for 10 minutes. Turn and broil for 10 minutes more (if the meat is thinner, reduce cooking time appropriately). Remove from broiler, tent lightly with tin foil and let rest for 10 minutes (the meat will continue to cook). Slice thinly against the grain and serve.

We serve three of us with this, then use leftovers for a stir fry.

Makes 6 to 8 servings

STIR FRY BEEF WITH BROCCOLI

This works well with the leftover rare London broil, especially since it repeats the flavors of the marinade. This also prevents the leftovers from becoming the same old same old.

1 bunch broccoli
2 cups of leftover London broil cut into
   1¹/₂ × ¹/₂ × ¹/₄-inch pieces.

1 piece of fresh ginger the size of a
   quarter, minced
¹/₂ cup green onions, sliced

Sauce:

¹/₂ cup beef broth
¹/₄ cup soy sauce
¹/₄ cup dry sherry or rice wine

¹/₄ cup packed brown sugar
A few drops of chili oil,
   to taste (optional)

Thickener:

1 T. cornstarch
1 T. water

Rinse the broccoli and break into florets. Cover and microwave on high for 3 minutes. Remove immediately, and rinse under cold running water to stop the cooking, or blanch the broccoli traditionally for 3 minutes in boiling water, then rinse.

Cut the ginger and green onions and set aside.

Mix together the sauce ingredients and set aside.

Mix together the thickener and set aside.

Heat 2 T. peanut oil in a non-stick frying pan. Stir in the green onions and ginger mixture. Stir fry until the aroma is released from the ginger and the mixture is slightly brown. Add the meat and mix. Add the prepared sauce and bring to a simmer. Simmer 1 minute, then add the broccoli and stir to coat with sauce. Push meat and vegetables aside and add the thickener to the sauce. Stir until thick. Cover, turn off heat and let stand for 2 minutes.

Substitutions: This also works with leftover roast pork or chicken. Use chicken broth in place of the beef broth. Or you can use ³/₄ lb. blanched snow peas or green beans in place of the broccoli.

Makes 4 to 6 servings

CROCK POT STEW

I could never find a recipe for bottom round roast that worked. So I relegated it to dog food (on sale, it is most reasonable). I tasted Patou's stew made in the Crock Pot, and found it passable. I tinkered with the recipe, and now we all eat this.

Place the following ingredients into a crockery slow cooker:

1 ³/₄-lb. bottom round roast, trimmed of fat and cut into 1¹/₂-inch cubes	1 cup liquid (beef broth, or half water and half wine)
3 carrots, finely diced	1 bay leaf
1 onion, thinly sliced	Pinch of thyme
2 cloves garlic, minced	Pinch of rosemary

Stir, cover and cook on high for 1 hour, then on low for 8 to 10 hours. Cool and remove bay leaf before serving.

If you have time, cool the liquid in the refrigerator and skim the fat from the top before thickening the gravy.

Please note: You also can make this traditionally by browning the meat first in a frying pan and then adding it to the Crock Pot. Then caramelize the onion in a little oil, add the garlic and other seasonings and cook to release the flavors. Add this to the Crock Pot. If you want to add whole baby carrots, cook them in a microwave or boil them until almost tender before you add them.

Makes 6 to 8 servings

🦴 🦴 🦴 🦴 🦴

CARAMELIZING ONIONS

All onions, even everyday yellow onions, are naturally high in sugar. Caramelizing them will bring out this sweetness.

Sauté the onions in vegetable oil, or a vegetable oil and butter combination, over medium heat. Stir occasionally. After about 5 minutes they will be a translucent tan color. Continue sautéing them for an additional 5 to 6 minutes. They will begin to turn a rich brown. This brown is the caramelized part. To speed the process, I will sometimes sprinkle a pinch of sugar over the onions to show them how I want them to go.

NEVER-FAIL MEATLOAF

Meatloaf takes time, but once prepared, with some Idaho or sweet potatoes in the oven with it, you can do other things. I like my meatloaf to be smooth, almost like a paté. I always make a double recipe of this, and use the leftovers for sandwiches and extra dinners for Patou. It also freezes well.

2 lb. ground beef (85 percent lean or better)
²/₃ cup low-fat milk
2 slices bread, torn in small pieces
1 egg
1 tsp. salt
Grinding of fresh pepper

¹/₂ tsp. dry mustard (or 1 tsp. regular mustard)
¹/₂ tsp. garlic powder
2 tsp. dry dehydrated onion
1 T. Worcestershire sauce
3 T. ketchup

Mix together everything except the beef and ketchup, until the bread is soaked and soft. Add meat and mix gently.

Prepare a loaf pan or other oven-proof pan by spraying it with aerosol vegetable spray. Place the meat in the pan and top with ketchup. Bake in pre-heated 350-degree oven for 1¹/₂ hours. Pour off any fat as soon as you take the meatloaf from the oven. Let it stand 10 minutes before slicing.

Makes 6 servings

IRISH STEW

3 lbs. stew meat or round roast, cut into 1¹/₂- to 2-inch cubes
2 T. vegetable oil
3 bay leaves
2 onions, sliced ¹/₄-inch thick
3 cloves garlic, chopped

¹/₂ tsp. dried thyme
3 T. flour
1 14-oz. can low-sodium beef stock
1 14-oz. can beer
1 lb. baby carrots
Salt and pepper

In a heavy Dutch oven over medium heat bring the beef stock and beer to a simmer.

Heat a non-stick frying pan. Brown the beef on all sides over high heat. You may have to do this in batches. If the pan residue gets too heavy, pour some of the stock and beer mixture in the pan to deglaze it, and pour this back into the Dutch oven. Deglaze the pan after all of the beef has been browned.

Heat the vegetable oil in the frying pan over high heat and add the sliced onions. Cook until they begin to brown and caramelize. Add the garlic and the bay leaves and cook, stirring until they release their aroma. Sprinkle the flour over the mixture and stir, incorporating it into the onion mixture.

Ladle some of the stock mixture into the frying pan to make certain that everything is mixed well. Add the contents of the frying pan to the beef. Add the baby carrots.

Cover and simmer for 2¹/₂ to 3 hours, or until the beef is very tender, adding liquid from the stock mixture as needed.

Add salt and pepper to taste before serving.

Makes 6 to 8 servings

SUPER BOWL BARBECUED BEEF

My mother was a veritable library of recipes. I would call her in Florida, tell her what I was trying to do, and she would supply me with three or four possible recipes. This particular one came as a result of my request for something for half time at a Super Bowl party we were having. It was perfect. It simmered away during the first half, then was ready when half time started. This is wonderful barbecued beef. But again, not forever. Patou happily finished all the leftovers.

1 4-lb. chuck roast or bottom/top round roast	¹/₂ cup cider vinegar
2 T. vegetable oil	1 tsp. salt
2 medium onions, sliced	2 T. Worcestershire sauce
1 clove garlic, minced	1 tsp. dry mustard
1 8-oz. can tomato sauce	¹/₄ tsp. pepper
1 6 oz. can tomato paste	2 bay leaves
²/₃ cup light brown sugar, packed	1 cup beef broth
	Parsley to garnish

Heat a heavy Dutch oven over medium high heat. Add the onion and cook until caramelized. Add the garlic and bay leaves and cook for one more minute. Add the tomato sauce, tomato paste, sugar, vinegar, salt, Worcester-shire sauce, mustard and pepper. Bring to a simmer and cover while you prepare the meat.

Slice the beef into 1×2×¹/₄-inch pieces. Brown the pieces on both sides in small batches in a large, hot non-stick skillet. Use ¹/₄ cup of the beef broth to deglaze the pan as necessary between the batches, pouring the deglazed juices into the sauce in the Dutch oven.

When all of the pieces have been browned and placed into the Dutch oven, lower the heat and simmer the beef for at least 2 hours, or until the meat is fork tender. Stir periodically and add the additional beef broth if necessary. Sprinkle with chopped parsley when ready to serve. Serve on soft sandwich rolls.

Makes 16 sandwich servings

Lamb

I love lamb. I love it roasted, stewed and skewered. I learned early on in my cooking career that a leg will do just fine for two people, and since I began feeding my dogs natural food, it disappears quickly. The full leg can be cut in half to provide a roast from one half (with leftovers the next day), and shish kabob cubes from the other half. And although I love lamb, I don't love it forever. Thankfully, we share these meals with our dog, who could eat lamb forever.

LEG OF LAMB

Roasts may not be fast food, but if you have time they need only simple and easy preparation, even on a harried day. Put the roast in the oven, then do other things.

With all of my roasts, I like to prepare the roast and get it in the oven. Then I prepare the accompaniments, which I also roast. I line them up then put them in the oven timed to come out 15 minutes after the roast is done.

1 5- or 6-lb. leg of lamb
2 cloves garlic, cut into thin slivers
Salt and pepper

Preheat oven to 375 degrees. Using a sharp knife, make about 10 slits 1 inch deep into the meaty part of the leg. Insert the slivered garlic into the cuts in the lamb. Lightly sprinkle the roast with salt and freshly ground pepper.

Place the leg, fat side up, in a shallow pan. Roast uncovered, without basting:

Rare	(130–135)	11–13 minutes per pound
Medium rare	(140–145)	13–15 minutes per pound
Medium	(150–160)	16–18 minutes per pound
Well done	(160–165)	18–20 minutes per pound

Let the roast rest 15 to 20 minutes before slicing.

Makes 10 servings

LAMB CURRY (FROM LEFTOVER LEG OF LAMB)

2 T. vegetable oil
1 large onion, sliced
3 large tart apples, cored and cubed
1/2 cup raisins
1 T. curry powder
1 T. lemon juice

Grated rind of half a lemon
2–3 T. flour
2 cups chicken stock or some leftover
    meat juices and enough chicken
    stock to make 2 cups
2 cups leftover lamb, cubed

In a large frying pan, sauté onion in oil until golden. Add the apple and garlic, and cook until warmed through. Blend in flour and curry powder, and stir to incorporate well.

Combine the lemon juice and the stock and stir gradually into the onion mixture. Stir in lemon rind and raisins. Cover and simmer for 30 minutes. Add cooked lamb and heat through.

Serve with rice.

Makes 4 servings

🦴 🦴 🦴 🦴 🦴

LAMB SHISH KEBOB

1¹/₂ lb. lamb shoulder or leg,
    cut into 1-inch cubes
1 small onion, thinly sliced
1 tsp. oregano
2 T. olive oil

1 pepper, red or green, cut into 1-inch
    squares
1 large sweet onion, cut into chunks
12 cherry tomatoes

Place the lamb, onion, oregano and olive oil into a bowl. Mix so that the onions and spices are well incorporated into the lamb. Refrigerate, covered, for 1 to 2 hours.

If you are using wooden skewers, soak the skewers in water for 1 hour.

Alternate the lamb, pepper and onion on skewers. Put tomatoes on separate skewers by themselves. Brush skewers with any remaining marinade in the bowl. Then discard the rest of the marinade.

Broil the lamb and pepper skewers 6 inches from the heat until brown on all sides (about 15 minutes). Broil the tomato skewers for about 5 minutes. Serve with rice.

Makes 4 generous servings

LAMB STEW

This dish was one added to my repertoire after we started feeding our dogs natural food. I will periodically go through stages when we add new vegetable or meat dishes to our regular fare. I am always trying to expand the kinds of foods we eat. The guilt-free way to experiment with a spice or herb or vegetable is by having a pet who is happy to eat your mistakes.

I vehemently dislike nutmeg, and avoided allspice as being of the same family. But I love lamb and cinnamon and tomatoes, so I gave it a try, all the time expecting the dogs to enjoy all of this. But I liked it as much as everyone else did. And this stew, if any is leftover, is better the second day.

3 lb. lamb, with all fat removed,
    cut in 1-inch cubes
3 T. vegetable oil
3 onions, peeled and coarsely
    chopped
1 scant tsp. paprika
1 scant tsp. allspice (or more,
    if you like)

¼ tsp. cinnamon
1 cinnamon stick
1 6-oz. can tomato paste
1½ cups water
¼ cup dry red wine
Salt and pepper

Heat oil in a large, non-stick frying pan. Brown lamb on all sides. Remove and keep warm. Add onions to remaining oil and brown well. Add paprika, allspice and cinnamon to onion mixture and cook until aromas are released. Return lamb to skillet and mix to incorporate with the spices. Slowly add the tomato paste and the water, and bring to a simmer.

Simmer, covered, for 1 hour or until the meat is very tender. Add the wine, cover and simmer for another 15 minutes. Adjust the seasonings, adding salt and pepper to taste. Serve over rice.

Makes 6 to 8 servings

Pork

Pork is not as fatty as it once was, making it an excellent choice for a healthy diet. It is also rich in B vitamins, zinc and iron. I have found that the larger cuts of pork are the tastier and moister cuts. Before we began sharing meals with our dogs, I would never consider a fresh ham as a possible dinner. But I've discovered it is excellent roasted, and provides wonderful company fare. Leftovers make the best stir fry dinners.

If I am porked out, I will freeze chunks of the pork to make a quick stir fry a few weeks later, or to use as a supplement to my dog's dinner if we are eating out and are short on leftovers.

FRESH HAM

¹/₂ fresh ham	¹/₂ tsp. whole dried rosemary, crushed
2 cloves garlic, cut into slivers	Salt and pepper

Preheat oven to 350 degrees. Leave a thin layer of fat on the pork. Pierce the flesh of the pork with a sharp knife, and insert garlic slivers into the meat. Sprinkle the fat with salt, pepper and crushed rosemary leaves.

Place ham, fat side up, in a roasting pan. Roast 30 to 35 minutes per pound, or until the internal temperature reaches 170 degrees.

Allow the roast to rest 15 to 20 minutes before carving.

Makes 10 to 12 generous servings, plus leftovers

BONELESS LOIN OF PORK

A smaller cut of pork, but an equally tasty one, is the boneless loin. Certain roasts, and this is one of them, will always have approximately the same diameter. It is this diameter that determines the length of time to roast this particular cut of meat. I have found 2 hours and 15 minutes at 375 degrees will bring the roast to 170 degrees internally. Resting it after it comes out of the oven will bring the temperature closer to 180 degrees.

1 3–4-lb. boneless loin of pork	¹/₂ cup chicken broth
2 cloves garlic, sliced the long way	Garlic salt
5 fresh sage leaves	Pepper

Preheat the oven to 375 degrees. Leave a thin layer of fat on the pork. Pierce the pork with a sharp knife, and insert garlic slivers from one clove into the meat. Between the two parts of the loin, insert the sage leaves and the rest of the garlic.

Sprinkle the fat with the garlic salt and pepper. Place the loin in a roasting pan, fat side up. Put the chicken broth in the pan. Roast 2 hours and 15 minutes, or until the internal temperature reaches 170 degrees.

Allow the roast to rest 15 to 20 minutes before slicing.

Makes 8 to 10 servings

Leftovers: You can make gravy with the defatted meat juices and reheat the roast this way. I find it less than satisfying. I tried using leftovers in fajitas, but they were nothing to write home about, either. I much prefer to use the leftover meat in stir fry dishes. Following are two of our favorites.

STIR FRY ROAST PORK

2 cups leftover pork, sliced into 1 × 2 × 1/8-inch pieces	1 lb. broccoli
	2 T. peanut oil

Cut and set aside:

1 tsp. ginger, chopped	1/2 red pepper, cut into thin strips (optional)
4 scallions, chopped into pea-size pieces, including the green part	

Sauce:

3 T. low-sodium soy sauce	2 T. oyster sauce
3 T. sherry or rice wine	1 tsp. sugar

Thickener:

2 T. water
1 T. cornstarch

Slice leftover pork and set aside.

Cut broccoli into florets. Wash, microwave on high for 3 minutes, and run under cold water to stop the cooking. Set aside.

Cut the red pepper, ginger and scallions, and set aside.

Mix the sauce ingredients and set aside.

Mix the cornstarch and water and set aside.

Heat the peanut oil over high heat in a wok or large, non-stick frying pan. Add the red pepper, scallion and ginger mixture and cook, stirring constantly, until the ginger is browned and releases its aroma. Add the broth and stir. Cover for 1 minute to cook the pepper.

Add the pork and stir gently. Slowly add the sauce mixture and stir. When the sauce mixture begins to bubble, stir in the cornstarch mixture and allow the sauce to thicken.

Add the broccoli and stir to incorporate into the mixture. Cover the pan and remove from the heat. Let the dish rest for 1 minute before serving.

Please note: This dish can be made with any fresh vegetables you have on hand. The following are some of your options:

¹/₂ head cauliflower, cut in florets and
    blanched
¹/₂ cup fresh or frozen peas

2 cups blanched green beans
¹/₂ lb. blanched snow peas

Makes 4 servings

ॐ ॐ ॐ ॐ ॐ

TWICE-COOKED PORK WITH SNOW PEAS

2 cups leftover pork, sliced into
    1 × 2 × ¹/₈-inch pieces
¹/₂ pound fresh snow peas
1 tsp. ginger, chopped

4 scallions, chopped into pea-size
    pieces, including the green part
2 T. peanut oil

Sauce:

¹/₄ cup low-sodium soy sauce
¹/₄ cup sherry or rice wine
¹/₂ cup chicken broth

2 T. brown sugar
2 T. Hoisin sauce
5 drops chili oil

Thickener:

1 T. cornstarch
3 T. water

Slice leftover pork and set aside.

Wash snow peas and remove stem end and string. Blanch for 30 seconds in boiling water, or microwave on high for 2 minutes. Rinse under cold running water to stop the cooking, and set aside.

Cut the ginger and scallions and set aside.

Mix the sauce ingredients and set aside.

Heat the peanut oil over high heat in a wok or large non-stick frying pan. Add the scallion and ginger mixture and cook, stirring constantly, until the ginger is browned and releases its aroma. Add the pork and stir gently. Slowly add the sauce mixture and stir. When the sauce mixture begins to bubble, stir in the cornstarch mixture, adding only enough to thicken the sauce. After the sauce is thickened, add the snow peas and stir to incorporate into the mixture. Cover the pan and remove from heat. Let the dish rest for 2 minutes before serving.

Makes 4 servings

Liver

SAUTÉED LIVER & ONIONS

My husband does not like liver, but I make this for Patou at least once a month. And many times if Ed will not be home for dinner, Patou will share this with me.

1 T. butter	2 large onions, thinly sliced
3 T. vegetable oil	1 lb. beef liver

Heat 1 T. butter and 1 T. oil in large, non-stick pan over medium heat. Add the onions. Sauté until they begin to caramelize and turn brown. Remove with a slotted spoon and set aside.

Turn the heat up to medium high and, if necessary, add the remaining oil. Rinse liver under cold running water and place the slices in a single layer into the hot pan. Cook 3 to 4 minutes on each side until the liver turns deep brown. It should be slightly pink in the center.

Put on a plate and cover with the onions.

Makes 2 servings for 1 Great Pyrenees
(or 1 serving for me and 1 plus leftovers for the Pyr)

Chapter 7

Main Dishes

CANINE LASAGNA

This dish was developed for my husband to feed our dogs when I had to be out of town for a few days. The first time that I made it and left it in the refrigerator, he thought it was his dinner and put it in the microwave. We all eat this now. The optional ingredients are for when I make this for all of us to share.

Meat Sauce:

1 small onion, diced
2 cloves garlic, minced
1 lb. ground turkey
1 16-oz. can tomato sauce or
    spaghetti sauce

$^1/_2$ tsp. oregano (optional)
$^1/_2$ tsp. basil (optional)
Pinch of fennel seeds (optional)
Olive oil

Sauté the onion and garlic together in a small amount of olive oil over medium heat until the onions are transparent. Add the ground turkey and cook well. Drain off any accumulated fat. Add the tomato or spaghetti sauce, and the oregano, basil and fennel seeds if desired. Cover and simmer on low for 15 minutes.

Cook According to Package Directions:

1 lb. macaroni

    Drain.

Mix Together:

1 lb. low-fat cottage cheese
1 egg
4 oz. grated mozzarella (optional)

Spray a 7 × 13-inch pan with aerosol oil. Put some sauce on the bottom of the pan. Pour half of the macaroni into the pan. Dollop and spread the egg and cheese mixture over macaroni. Using a slotted spoon, spoon about ³/₄ of the meat mixture over the cheese. Layer on the rest of the macaroni. Pour the remaining meat sauce on top.

Top with:

4 oz. grated mozzarella (optional)
Parmesan and more oregano (optional)

Cover with foil and bake in preheated 350-degree oven for 30 to 40 minutes (depending on the shape of the pan). Remove foil for the last 10 minutes of baking.

With a salad and some French bread, this serves the three of us very well. It can also be prepared ahead and frozen or refrigerated. Add 10 to 15 minutes baking time for the refrigerated dish, and 45 to 60 minutes more for the frozen.

SPAGHETTI AND MEATBALLS

When my mother was newly married she had the good fortune to live in an ethnically diverse neighborhood. Her neighbors on either side were first-generation Americans—a young Italian family on one side and a Polish family on the other. My mother, of Lithuanian descent, shared her recipes with them, and they shared theirs with her.

My mother taught me this recipe the same way she learned it from her neighbors: by standing over my shoulder with hands-on instructions—too much, a little more, not that way, and so on. I have tried to quantify these ingredients for you. You may have to tinker with the amounts, but try the recipe initially as formulated. The effect is always the same: the ultimate comfort food.

Spaghetti and meatballs is one of my family's favorite foods. I have yet to share this meal with a human or a dog who did not like it. And because this one cooks for a while, the entire house is permeated with the sweet smells of the browned garlic and tomatoes. By the time dinner is served, even the most finicky eater (human or dog) is ready.

Prepare the Sausage:

1 lb. Italian sweet sausage, cut into 3-inch pieces

Put the sausage into a non-stick frying pan with enough water to cover the bottom of the pan. Sauté over medium high heat until it begins to cook (change color) on one side. Turn sausage over and cook on other side. Drain any water and fat from the pan and lower heat to medium low.

Pierce sausages (I use a poultry skewer, but corn on the cob holders will work) to allow the fat to drip into the pan. Let the sausages brown lightly on one side. Turn sausages over and pierce the other side. Allow sausages to brown lightly again on this side. When well browned, remove sausages from the pan and allow them to drain on paper toweling until ready to put in the tomato sauce.

Prepare the Meatballs:

1¼ lb. ground beef,
    as lean as possible
1 clove garlic, crushed
1 large egg
¼ cup water

⅓ cup Italian-style bread crumbs
    (or regular bread crumbs with a
    pinch of oregano, basil and
    Parmesan cheese)
Pinch of salt (optional)
Freshly ground black pepper to taste

Gently mix the ingredients together. The meatball mix should begin to stick to itself rather than to your hand. If the mix is sticky, add a little more bread crumbs. But go easy, because you want meatballs, not bread-crumb balls.

Prepare the Sauce:

1 T. olive oil
3 cloves garlic
1 28-oz. can tomato puree and
    ½ of this can filled with water
1 6-oz. can of tomato paste and a full
    can of water

1 8-oz. can tomato sauce
1 scant tsp. salt
3 T. sugar
Freshly ground pepper to taste
2 tsp. dried basil or
    2 T. fresh basil

In heavy Dutch oven, heat the olive oil. Lightly brown the garlic cloves. Do not allow them to burn. (If they burn, discard and begin again with new oil and garlic.)

Add the puree, paste, sauce and appropriate amounts of water. Stir together and season with salt, sugar and pepper. Taste and adjust the seasonings. Depending on the acid content of the tomatoes, you may need to add additional sugar.

Bring the sauce to a simmer.

Form your meatballs into $1^1/_2$- to 2-inch balls. Wet your hands under cold running water after each second or third meatball that you make. (This helps keep the meatballs fluffy.) Gently drop the meatballs into the simmering sauce. Add the sausage, spooning the sauce over the sausage so that it is totally covered. Bring the sauce to a slow simmer and cover either with a spatter shield or partly cover with the pot lid for $1^1/_2$ hours. Periodically, using a wooden spoon, gently lift the meatballs and sausage from the bottom of the pot to keep them from sticking. Handle the meatballs lightly, as they are very tender and break easily.

Five minutes before the end of the cooking time add the basil. Stir gently to incorporate.

This will hold, covered (depending on the type of pot) at least $^1/_2$ hour or up to 1 hour before serving.

Ladle some sauce onto the cooked and drained pasta, and stir to distribute. Put pasta into individual serving bowls and top with a meatball or sausage and some sauce.

Serve with freshly grated parmesan or asiago cheese.

Enough for 4 servings, plus leftovers

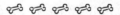

CHICKEN FAJITAS

This goes into the category of last-minute preparation. And if I didn't love them so much, I would never bother with the preparation.

2 T. vegetable oil	$1^1/_2$ lb. boneless chicken breasts
4 onions, thinly sliced	Ground cumin
2 large red bell peppers, thinly sliced	Oregano
Salt and pepper to taste	$^1/_2$ lime
2 cloves garlic, minced	1 pkg. large flour tortillas

To Garnish:

Shredded mild cheese (such as Monterey Jack)	Salsa
Shredded lettuce	Chopped tomatoes

Heat a large, non-stick skillet. Put in oil and then add the onions. Cook until well browned and caramelized. Stir periodically to prevent burning. When adequately browned, season liberally with the oregano and ground cumin, salt and pepper. Add the red peppers on top of the onions and sprinkle with the garlic and some additional oregano and cumin. Lower the heat to medium-low and cover while you prepare the chicken. Check on the peppers periodically so they don't burn.

Cut any excess fat from the chicken breasts and either flatten them or cut the filets out of them so that they will cook evenly. Sprinkle one side of each breast with the oregano and the cumin.

When the peppers are cooked to your satisfaction (the smaller they are cut, the faster they will cook) remove the peppers and onions into a heat-proof bowl.

Turn the heat up high under the frying pan and put in the chicken, seasoned side down (you don't need to add any additional fat). Season the other side with the oregano and cumin. When the first side of the chicken has browned, turn it over and brown the other side.

When both sides are browned, return the pepper and onion mixture to the frying pan, and cook over medium heat for 5 minutes. Squeeze half of the lime over the mixture. Then turn the heat to low.

This can be held at this stage on low for at least ¹/₂ hour.

You can heat the tortillas any number of ways. I put them on a plate, cover them with a wet piece of paper towel and microwave on high for 1 minute. You can also heat them in a conventional oven in tin foil at 350 degrees for 15 minutes.

Assembly: Cut the chicken into bite-sized pieces. If you have hands-on family or guests, they can assemble the tortillas themselves or you can do it for them.

Place some salsa on each tortilla, followed by the chicken and the pepper and onion mixture. Roll the tortilla and put on a plate. Sprinkle with the cheese and top with the lettuce and tomatoes. Serve immediately.

For Patou, I omit the salsa and dispense with the rolling. Simply tear the tortilla into small pieces.

Makes 6 to 8 generous fajitas

TURKEY CHILI

This is one of those recipes that makes me glad to have a dog to share a meal with. My husband does not like beans, and it always seemed like such an extravagance to prepare this just for me. Then I discovered that Patou thought chili was wonderful.

While there are adequate spices in the recipe, I err on the light side of the heat. I add my hot sauce at the table, and serve Patou's chili with rice to temper it.

2 T. vegetable oil
2 medium onions, diced
3 cloves garlic, minced
2 lbs. ground turkey
1 28-oz. can plum tomatoes, seeded and diced (reserve the juice)
1 T. chili powder

1 tsp. oregano
1/2 tsp. cumin
1 T. brown sugar
1/2 tsp. salt
2 16-oz. cans small red beans, drained and rinsed
non-fat plain yogurt as garnish (optional)

Heat the oil in a Dutch oven over medium high heat. Sauté the onions until they begin to turn brown and caramelize. Add the garlic, and stir to incorporate. Add the ground turkey and fry, breaking it up into small pieces, until cooked through. Drain any accumulated fat.

Add the diced plum tomatoes, the chili powder, oregano and cumin. Stir to incorporate. Bring to a boil, reduce heat, cover and simmer for 1 hour. Stir periodically and add any of the reserved tomato juice if the mixture becomes too dry. After an hour, add the beans to the chili mixture. Cover and simmer for another 15 minutes.

Serve with extra hot sauce and a dollop of yogurt.

Offer your human company some chopped raw sweet onion and grated cheese on the side.

Makes 6 to 8 servings

EGGPLANT PARMESAN

I love eggplant, and so have all of my dogs. They also love the spaghetti sauce and the cheeses, so this is a real winner with them. I used to fry each piece of eggplant in oil, drain on paper towels, then layer and bake. But being careful about eating too much fat and never having enough time in the day, I developed this method of preparing the eggplant.

I much prefer the fried version, but if it is a choice of no eggplant parmesan or this totally baked version, I opt for this one. And because this recipe takes minutes to prepare and then bakes for an hour, I use that time to take my dog and myself for a walk.

1 medium eggplant	1 32-oz. jar spaghetti sauce
2 eggs	1 16-oz. package part-skim
2 T. milk	mozzarella cheese, shredded
1–2 cups Italian seasoned	Oregano and Parmesan
bread crumbs	cheese to taste

Preheat oven to 350 degrees. Spray a 7 × 11-inch or similar pan with aerosol vegetable oil spray.

Peel and slice one eggplant into ¼-inch rounds. Beat milk and eggs together in a shallow bowl or pie plate, and pour the bread crumbs into another plate. (If you don't have Italian bread crumbs, add oregano, parmesan cheese and garlic powder to regular bread crumbs.)

Dip the eggplant into the egg mixture to coat, then into the bread crumbs to cover. Place the slices in the prepared oven-proof pan, overlapping slightly. When the first layer is complete, spray the eggplant with more aerosol vegetable spray. Cover the layer with half of the spaghetti sauce and half of the shredded cheese. Sprinkle with some oregano and parmesan cheese.

Repeat the procedure with the rest of the eggplant, creating another layer, spraying that, then topping with the rest of the sauce and some oregano.

Cover with tin foil and bake in the preheated oven for 1 hour or until completely cooked (no resistance when the eggplant is pierced with a fork). Remove the tin foil and top with the remaining mozzarella and parmesan cheese, and return to the oven for an additional 5 minutes or until the cheese is melted. Remove from the oven, then let rest covered with the tin foil for 10 to 15 minutes before cutting.

Serve with a tossed salad and some French bread to complete the meal.

Makes 4 servings

OMELETS

Omelets can make a quick supper or a super brunch. The latest findings are that eggs are not as bad cholesterol-wise for you as we once thought, and the yolk contains nutrients not readily available elsewhere. Also, eggs are not expensive, so they are a perfect food to learn on. And your pet will love his cheese omelet, even if it is not perfectly turned. Better still, eggs and individually packaged cheese slices keep well in your refrigerator and are always available.

Raw eggs, like chicken, can harbor salmonella bacteria, so don't cross-contaminate. Keep the plates and utensils that come in contact with raw eggs away from the serving plates and forks.

1 T. butter
3 eggs beaten with 1 T. water

2 slices of individually
wrapped cheese

Heat the butter in a 9-inch non-stick frying pan over medium high heat.

Beat the eggs and water together until fluffy. Pour the egg mixture into the pan and allow it to sit there for a minute, or until the edges begin to become opaque. Lift the edges to let the uncooked egg seep under the cooked egg. When most of the egg has been cooked, place the cheese on half of the omelet. Flip the untopped half onto the cheese. Let it rest in the pan for about 30 seconds, then slip onto a plate to serve.

Optional Fillings: The no-brainer omelet in our house is the one made with individually wrapped American cheese slices. I can get one of these onto the table in less than 5 minutes, starting with a closed refrigerator door.

You can make this with any other cheese, but the harder cheeses like cheddar should be shredded. I avoid Swiss, as it's too stringy. Use about 1/3 cup shredded cheese per omelet. Salsa can be added before you add the cheese. Or forget the cheese and just use the salsa. Two tablespoons can really spice up the dish.

Leftover Chinese food can also be used as a filling, as can almost any leftover vegetable. I like leftover mushrooms, or tomato-based vegetable combinations like ratatouille or baked yellow squash with tomatoes. If you are using a lot of filling in the eggs, or the filling just came out of the refrigerator, you may want to heat it up in a microwave before adding it to the eggs.

🦴 🦴 🦴 🦴 🦴

FISH MEUNIERE

I have not had great luck buying fish other than live lobster and frozen shrimp. I rarely make fish, but prefer to eat it out. However, my most successful home-cooked fish dinners are the ones made with fresh-from-the-water fish given to us by friends or neighbors. We were introduced to perch by an experienced ice fisherman in New York, and sea trout by a neighbor at our marina in New Jersey. Both of these fish lend themselves to the following method of cooking, as do other thin white fish fillets like flounder or sole.

1¹/₂ lbs. small fish fillets	1 cup flour
1 cup milk	Salt and pepper
1 tsp. red pepper sauce	Oil and butter, in equal parts, for frying

Cover fillets with milk. Add enough red pepper sauce to turn the milk a light to medium pink. Put the fish and milk mixture in the refrigerator for ¹/₂ hour, or as long as 1 hour. When you're ready to cook the fish, put 2 T. each of oil and butter in a heavy non-stick frying pan. Heat over medium-high heat.

Add salt and pepper to the flour for dredging. Remove fillets from the milk mixture and shake off excess liquid. Dredge in flour, covering both sides, and place immediately into the frying pan. Continue with the rest of the fillets. Do not crowd the pan. Fry until golden on one side, then turn and fry on the other. These fillets are very tender, so handle them carefully. When browned on both sides, remove from the pan to a plate and serve with a wedge of lemon.

Makes 4 servings

BAKED FISH

Larger fish fillets do not lend themselves to frying. Instead, I bake them with butter and lemon. This is particularly good with a salmon fillet.

Per Serving:

1 4–6 oz. fillet
1 T. butter

1 T. lemon juice
Sprinkling of paprika

Measure the depth of the fish at the thickest part. Place the fish in the smallest oven-proof dish that can accommodate it. Pour the butter and the lemon juice over it, and sprinkle the top with paprika.

Bake in a 400-degree oven for 12 minutes per inch of thickness. The fish should be completely opaque when it is cooked.

Serve with lemon wedges.

MANICOTTI

Once you learn how to make crepes, manicotti is only a short step away.

1 recipe of Lisa's Mom's Crepes
(You'll find the recipe in
Chapter 9, on page 95.)
1 lb. part-skim ricotta cheese

1 8-oz. package mozzarella cheese,
shredded
1/2 cup parmesan cheese
Homemade or prepared tomato sauce

Mix the ricotta cheese with 3/4 of the mozzarella. Place the most attractive side of the crepe down on the work surface. Place about 1/4 cup of the cheese mixture onto the lower third of the crepe. Roll the crepe from the filled side to the unfilled side.

Place seam side down in an oven-proof baking dish. Continue with the rest of the crepes. When all the crepes are rolled, cover with tomato sauce and the remaining mozzarella and bake, lightly covered with foil, for 35 minutes at 350 degrees.

Makes 4 to 6 servings as a side dish

Chapter 8

Vegetables

Stay Home and Tend Your Garden . . .

If I had my way, I would be able to look out my window and see a huge, well-tended vegetable garden. What a joy it would be to step out my back door, select some vegetables and herbs, and cook.

But getting older has taught me to accept my limitations. I do not like to garden. I tried it, and I could not force myself to enjoy it. I have a small patch of herbs that emerges every spring like a gift from the earth, but I don't garden. I shop for my vegetables. It is my responsibility to find the best, safest and freshest produce available.

Fortunately for my dogs and me, farmers' markets are making a comeback. Buying produce directly from the people who grow it is almost as good as cultivating it yourself.

If you do not have access to a farmers' market or fruit stand, seek out those places where those who purchase and handle the vegetables take the greatest care. Take the time to look for a good vegetable supplier. If you can, try different vendors on different days. At one local grocery store the vegetables look ragged on Tuesday but wonderful on Friday afternoons. I shop there on Fridays.

Count on shopping at least twice a week for fresh vegetables. You will lose the sweet freshness of these vegetables if they remain too long in your refrigerator, and a full week's worth of fresh vegetables takes up a lot of room.

If you cannot shop twice a week, buy fresh vegetables for the first half of the week and either count on vegetables such as broccoli and beets, which store well, or use acceptable frozen vegetables such as peas or kernel corn to make up the rest of the week.

MICROWAVING VEGETABLES

I cook almost all of our vegetables in the microwave. I just rinse them and set them down to drain for a few minutes. Along with the water that still clings to them after that, I put them in a microwaveable bowl with a loose fitting lid. The cooking time depends on the wattage of your oven and the quantity of vegetables to be cooked. My microwave is 600 watts, and 7 minutes for a pound of prepared green beans will produce a wonderfully tender, crisp vegetable.

Practice with your microwave to find out what works for you in the quantities you need for your family. Microwaving vegetables is not a science. Err on the underdone side if you have to.

I will also precook most of the vegetables I use in a stir fry. Pre-microwave, I would parboil them for 3 minutes in rapidly boiling water, then cool them quickly under cold running water. I now microwave the same vegetables for 3 to 3½ minutes, remove them and cool them rapidly under cold running water. The result is the same, but microwaving is much faster and easier.

Eat with the season. Eat asparagus, tomatoes and sweet corn until you are almost sick of them. These vegetables are best when fresh and locally grown. Eat enough so that you won't crave them for the rest of the year. Eating this way will not provide you and your dog with a daily balanced diet, but over the course of a year it will be as well balanced as any. And ultimately better.

Eat fruits and vegetables produced in or close to your home state. Don't be afraid to ask where a particular product has been grown. One of my markets labels most of the produce for state or country of origin. If not labeled, a good green grocer knows and can tell you.

Where possible, avoid imported fruits and vegetables. The U.S. bans certain insecticides and fungicides that are used legally in countries whose vegetables we import. Not all pesticides can be totally removed by washing, and any residue on the fruit and vegetables can be ingested by you and your dog.

Developing nations, while they may have ideal growing climates for many vegetables, may have primitive sanitation. Frequently, their standards of hygiene are different from ours. These differences are directly attributable to the salmonella contamination of imported cantaloupes in 1991. Cross contamination is not uncommon.

Always give preference to vegetables grown in the USA. With the agricultural activity in California and Florida, we have a full range of vegetables available throughout most of the year.

Err on the safe side. Wash all fruits and vegetables well. If you are not certain of the country of origin, and if you won't be peeling or cooking it, don't buy it.

Make the time to learn about, purchase and prepare fresh vegetables. Your mother was right: They really are good for you. Even if you don't want to eat them yourself, take good care of your canine friend. Serve some fresh vegetables with each meal.

The following are some common vegetables, with notes on seasonal availability and what to look for when buying them.

Asparagus

Asparagus means spring can't be far away. In mid-March we see the first of this vegetable from California. For three months it is available in abundance as the shoots grow closer to home.

Select smooth, thin spears with tight, dark heads. If you will not be using them immediately, trim the bottoms and stand upright in water in the refrigerator, lightly covered with a plastic bag.

When you are ready to prepare them, rinse them under running water and snap the tough bottoms off. Place them in a frying pan and sauté in a quarter cup of water for 4 to 6 minutes or until tender crisp. Or tie the spears together and place, heads up, in an asparagus cooker. Add enough water to reach 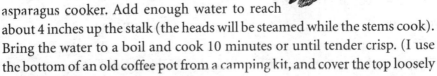 about 4 inches up the stalk (the heads will be steamed while the stems cook). Bring the water to a boil and cook 10 minutes or until tender crisp. (I use the bottom of an old coffee pot from a camping kit, and cover the top loosely with tin foil.)

Grilling is another option, especially if you have the grill going for something else. Microwave the asparagus for 3 minutes (to "parboil"). While still warm, dress the asparagus with a little olive oil. Grill, turning frequently, until the spears are marked with the grill lines and are tender.

Beans

Green Beans

Green beans are a summer crop, and although they are available most of the year,
they are best from mid-summer to the first
frost. Select green beans that are plump and
free of brown spots. If you can, snap one
in half. It should make a sharp cracking

sound. If it bends, pass them up. If you have the choice, select the smaller
beans. The larger ones may be fibrous and woody.

Cut off the tip and tails, and if they are large, snap the beans into 2-inch
pieces. Rinse, and put them in a microwave-safe bowl with a loose lid. Microwave 1 lb. on high for 7 minutes. Uncover and serve immediately. Or drop
them into boiling water and, when the water returns to the boil, cook for
7 minutes.

Treat yellow beans and wax beans the same way. The only difference is
that the color should be a pale yellow, and they are best eaten when their
tips and tails are slightly tinged with green.

If you cannot get fresh beans, your dog may accept the frozen variety.
But after you taste the fresh, you'll pass on the frozen. (And never mind
those in the can.)

GREEN BEAN CASSEROLE

*It would not be Thanksgiving dinner without this casserole, a recipe that I
understand was developed by a soup company to sell its product.*

*Using fresh green beans really raises the level of this dish, and while I have used
fresh mushrooms and cream, the memories were formed with this combination:*

1 lb. prepared green beans	1 T. Worcestershire sauce
1 can cream of mushroom soup	1 can French-fried onion rings
1/2 of the soup can filled with milk	

Cook the greens beans about 3 minutes and immediately run under cold
water to stop the cooking process. (This can be done early in the day.) Put
the beans in an oven-proof casserole dish. Mix together the soup, milk,
Worcestershire sauce and half the onion rings. Mix this into the beans.
Cover with foil and bake at 350 degrees for 25 minutes. Uncover and top
with the remaining onion rings. Bake for 5 minutes longer.

Makes 4 to 6 servings

WAX BEANS & SPIKE

Spike is a melange of spices available in most health food stores. It adds a wonderful flavor to some otherwise drab foods. My friend Michelle gave me my first jar. At that time Lisa lived with us, and we "spiked" everything. This was one of the more successful dishes.

1 lb. prepared wax beans
2 T. butter
Spike

Prepare the wax beans the same way you would the green beans. When they are completely cooked and still hot, add small pieces of the butter to the beans and sprinkle liberally with the spike. Cover the beans and let them rest for 2 minutes before serving.

Makes 4 servings

Beets

You can eat both the beet greens and the beet root. If you are looking for the greens, select the smaller, younger greens with bright green tops and narrow ribs. If you want the beets and the greens for the dog, select small to medium, well-shaped beets of similar size. Remove the greens from the beet root before storing the roots in the refrigerator. Leave about half an inch of the stem on to keep them from bleeding.

Most of the time there are not enough greens for everyone, so I will usually quickly rinse the greens and sauté them with a little garlic and olive oil for Patou. I find these a little bitter for me, but he thinks they are great.

To prepare the beet roots, wash them well and place in a pan with cold water to cover. Bring to a boil and boil gently for about 1 hour or until the beets are tender when pierced with a fork. When the beets are cool enough to handle, run them under cold water. With a sharp knife, slice off the tops and bottoms. The skin should slip right off (and your hands and sink will turn red).

You can slice and serve them as is, or try one of the following recipes.

QUICK BEETS IN ORANGE SAUCE

1 bunch beets, cooked and
   cut into rounds

1 T. butter
¼ cup orange marmalade

While the beets are still hot, stir in the butter and the marmalade. Cover and let them rest for 5 minutes before serving.

Makes 4 servings

BEET SALAD

My mother made this in the winter, when it would add much needed color to the table. And I love the pink onions. Neither my husband nor Patou will eat this, but I used to share it with Patou's dam (who would only eat the beets), when she was still alive. Now I will occasionally just make it for me, but I always remember Cher when I eat it.

1 lb. beets, cooked and sliced
1 onion, sliced into
   rounds and separated
½ cup vinegar

½ cup water
2 T. sugar
4 cloves
4 peppercorns

Mix all of the ingredients together and refrigerate for at least 24 hours.

Makes 6 servings as a side salad

Broccoli

Broccoli is readily available year-round, but it is best in the fall, winter and early spring. It is particularly welcome at this time, when there is a paucity of other green vegetables.

Most dogs and people really like their vegetables crisp, so select dark green heads with small, tight buds. If the buds are yellow or open, the broccoli is too old. Check the cut end to see if it is dried out or limp. If the stalk is limp and the florets look okay, it is okay to buy if you will use it immediately. Really fresh broccoli can be kept in the refrigerator lightly wrapped in a plastic bag for up to one week without loss of flavor or texture.

To prepare broccoli, rinse under cold water and break or cut into florets. You may elect to coarsely peel the stems and slice the results into ¹/₄-inch rounds to give the added variety of taste and crunch. Microwave, covered, on high for 7 minutes, uncover and serve immediately. Or steam for 10 minutes. If you are using this in stir fry, microwave for 3 minutes or until you begin to smell the broccoli cooking. Remove and cool under cold running water.

I rarely do anything with the broccoli except serve it. If I get fancy, it may get a sprinkling of freshly grated Parmesan, but usually it stands alone. I consider broccoli the original fast food fresh vegetable. It can go from refrigerator to table in less than 10 minutes.

Brussels Sprouts

Brussels sprouts are at their best in late fall and early winter, right after the first frost. These little cabbage wannabees are, like broccoli, members of the nutritionally powerful cruciferous family. Brussels sprouts are wonderfully nutty when tiny, fresh and cooked until just barely tender.

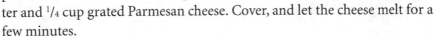

Select small ones of similar size, with no yellow. Trim the bottoms and cut a cross into the core. Drop them into a large quantity of rapidly boiling salted water, and cook 5 to 7 minutes or until just tender when pierced with a fork. Drain and put in 1 T. butter and ¹/₄ cup grated Parmesan cheese. Cover, and let the cheese melt for a few minutes.

If you cannot get good, small, fresh Brussels sprouts, pass on them. Don't even consider frozen ones.

Cabbage

Another member of the cruciferous family, cabbage comes in assorted colors and sizes. It is available from early summer through the winter, and is an excellent source of vitamins C and E. Look for cabbage heads that are tight, firm and heavy for their size. Their outer leaves should be shiny and crisp and show no sign of discoloration or cracking.

BRAISED CABBAGE

This is perfect with any roast pork dish. Before the food processor was invented it was time consuming, but not anymore. The cabbage reduces considerably, so you may choose to double the recipe. If you do, start with the butter and layer the cabbage, followed by the flour and salt. Then layer another head of cabbage, followed by the flour and salt.

1 head of cabbage, shredded	1 T. sugar
2 T. butter	1½ T. cider vinegar
1 T. flour	¾ cup water or stock
1 tsp. salt	

Melt the butter in the bottom of a heavy Dutch oven. Put the cabbage on top of the butter. Sprinkle with the salt and flour. Cover with the water or stock. Bring to a boil, lower the heat and cover. Braise for 1½ to 2 hours. Stir occasionally, and if necessary add more liquid. Add the sugar and vinegar just before serving.

Makes 4 servings

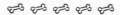

SWEET & SOUR RED CABBAGE

This is great with German pot roast, and although one head makes a lot, the vinegar allows it to keep easily in the refrigerator for a week. I was pleasantly surprised that Patou liked this.

1 medium head red cabbage, finely shredded	½ cup of red wine vinegar
3 tart apples (such as Granny Smiths)	½ cup red wine
2 onions, sliced	½ cup firmly packed brown sugar
2 T. butter or vegetable oil	2 chicken or beef bouillon cubes
	Salt and pepper to taste

Heat butter in a Dutch oven. Add the onion and cook until wilted and soft. Add the rest of the ingredients and stir well. Cover and cook on low for 1 hour. Stir occasionally, and add a few drops of water if necessary.

Makes 6 to 8 servings

Carrots

While carrots are a summer vegetable, their abundance in the winter, thanks to California farmers, brightens a winter roast or stew. Look for firm, crisp carrots of uniform size with unblemished skin. If the tops are still on, they should be bright green and fresh looking. Remove the tops before storing in the refrigerator. They will easily keep for more than a week.

I use carrots liberally in soups and stews, but never serve just plain carrots. Neither my husband nor my dog will eat them. If the carrots are cooked with a roast, my dog will eat them. Otherwise, Patou will push them out of his bowl onto the floor. My husband is more polite.

So with the variety available, I feel we can pass on the carrots as long as we make up for this vegetable by eating plenty of other vegetables that we like, such as sweet potatoes and broccoli.

Cauliflower

Select cauliflower with bright white, dense heads free of any brown discoloration or shaved spots. What leaves are still attached should be a fresh looking light green. Store in a loose plastic bag for no more than 4 days in the refrigerator. After this time, the flavor will become stronger.

To microwave, wash the head of cauliflower and break into florets. Microwave, covered, on high for about 7 minutes. Remember, the cauliflower will continue to cook even after it is removed from the microwave, so if it is still a little crisp, let it sit covered in the bowl for a few more minutes. Top with butter and fresh chives, Parmesan cheese or a light vinaigrette dressing (recipe on page 81).

VITAMINS AND MINERALS IN COMMON VEGETABLES

Asparagus	Vitamins A, B complex and C; potassium, manganese, phospherous and iron
Beans, green	Vitamins A, B complex and C; chlorophyll, calcium, phosphorus, copper and cobalt
Beets	Vitamins A, B complex and C; calcium, phosphorus, sodium, potassium, iron and magnesium
Broccoli	Vitamins A and C; calcium, selenium, phosphorus and potassium
Brussels sprouts	Vitamins A and C, riboflavin; iron, potassium and fiber
Carrots	Betacarotene, Vitamins B complex, C, D, E and K; iron, calcium, phosphorus, sodium, potassium, magnesium, manganese, sulfur, copper and iodine
Corn and cornmeal	Vitamins A, B, C , K and E; potassium, magnesium and fiber; Cornmeal enriched with lysine makes a complete protein.
Dark green, leafy vegetables	Vitamins A, C, F, K and E; chlorophyll, iron, magnesium, calcium, manganese, potassium. The vegetables with the darkest, most intense color usually contain the highest levels of nutrients.
Garlic	Vitamin A, iodine, phosphorous, potassium and selenium
Green peas	Carotene, vitamin C and high amounts of fiber
Olive oil and other vegetable oils	Vitamins D and F
Potatoes	Very high in vitamins A, B and C; potassium and iron
Squash, summer	Respectable amounts of vitamins A and C; phosphorous, potassium and calcium
Squash, winter	High in vitamin A; the deep orange varieties, like butternut, are high in beta-carotene and rich in iron and potassium.
Sweet peppers	Sweet peppers contain more vitamin C than citrus fruits, especially the red ones; they are also rich in vitamin A.
Sweet potatoes	Probably the healthiest of all vegetables; an excellent source of vitamins A and C; calcium, iron, folate and copper
Tomatoes	Moderate amounts of vitamins A and C; potassium, phosphorous, iodine and selenium

FRIED CAULIFLOWER

This recipe takes 30 minutes from the time the florets hit the pan until they are ready to serve.

1 head cauliflower	1 tsp. dried oregano
2 T. olive oil	1/2 tsp. ground cumin
2 T. butter	1 T. water
1 clove garlic, minced	

Rinse the head of cauliflower and dry well. Break it into florets. Heat the olive oil and butter in a large skillet over medium high heat. Cook the florets until nicely browned on all sides. When brown, sprinkle with the garlic, oregano and cumin. Add the water to the bottom of pan and continue to cook, steaming the cauliflower. Cover and reduce heat to low.

The entire process of browning and steaming takes approximately 30 minutes. Shake the pan to distribute the seasonings. Pour into a bowl and pour the pan juices on top.

Please note: I use oregano and cumin in this because I like that combination of flavors. You or your dogs may prefer some other combination, perhaps basil and roasted walnuts, or just lots of freshly chopped parsley.

Makes 6 servings

Corn

Corn is my favorite vegetable. And corn is usually not completely broken down in the digestive tracts of dogs or humans, so it is a particularly good food for dogs on weight-loss diets. They usually love the taste, and when they eat it they feel full, but they do not end up with a lot of calories from the corn.

In the summer I make a meal of good, fresh corn. The best guarantee of top-quality corn is to know your vegetable market, its sources and its ability to keep the freshly picked corn cold. Look for moist cut ends on the stalks and husks that are still fresh. The kernels should all be about the same size and in even rows. Fresh corn will have a pearly luminescence. If it lacks the glow or fullness, or otherwise looks dry, pass it up.

Again, I only buy corn when it's in season locally, and then only from a farmer who consistently supplies excellent quality. Otherwise, frozen corn is the better choice.

If you are using the ears the day they are purchased, corn can be stored as is in the refrigerator. If you want to keep them for one or two days, husk them and put them in a zipper-seal plastic bag and get as much air out as possible. Store them in the coolest part of your refrigerator.

To prepare the corn, husk and remove the silk. Fill a large stock pot with cold water and bring to a boil. Add sugar (I usually add about ¼ cup). When the water is boiling rapidly, drop in the corn, cover and cook for about 6 to 7 minutes (usually the water will boil again after about 4 minutes). Turn off the heat and keep the corn covered. It can stay covered this way for about 15 minutes.

My parents' German Shepherd Dog would hold the corn cob between her two front paws and carefully eat the kernels. My dogs loved corn so much that they would start eating the husk as well, which is way too much roughage for any dog. It would happen so fast that we could blink and half the cob would be gone before we could take it away. Now we just scrape the corn off the cob and sprinkle it over their food.

Eggplant

Eggplant lends itself to the robust flavors of garlic, tomatoes and basil. And while I cook most vegetables on the underdone side, you cannot do this with eggplant. Eggplant is at its best in August and September. Choose smaller produce with firm flesh and shiny skin. Peel the skin or not, as you choose. Because eggplant acts like a sponge around oil, do not fry it. There are plenty of other ways to cook it.

MIXED GRILLED VEGETABLES

In the summer when the grill is going, make this vegetable side dish before the meat goes on.

1 red pepper, roasted and peeled	¼ cup fresh basil leaves, torn
1 large sweet onion	2 small sprigs of fresh thyme
1 eggplant, sliced into	(If you don't have fresh basil or
¼ inch lengths	thyme, do not use dried; just omit
1 summer squash, quartered	them.)
lengthwise	Salt and pepper to taste
1 clove garlic, minced	Vinaigrette dressing (recipe below)

Roast and peel the red pepper, and cut into a small dice. Halve the onion and skewer it together. Brush the onion, eggplant and squash with olive oil, and season lightly with salt and pepper. Grill these vegetables until nicely browned and cooked through.

Mince the garlic and add to the bowl with the red pepper and torn basil leaves and thyme. Roughly chop the eggplant, onion and squash, and add to the red pepper mixture. Lightly dress with the vinaigrette dressing. Serve warm or at room temperature.

Makes 4 servings

ॐ ॐ ॐ ॐ ॐ

VINAIGRETTE DRESSING

¹/₂ cup olive oil	1 tsp. sugar
¹/₄ cup red wine vinegar	1 tsp. Dijon mustard
¹/₂ tsp. salt	Pepper to taste

Mix all of the ingredients together. Store in a glass jar in the refrigerator. Bring to room temperature before using.

ॐ ॐ ॐ ॐ ॐ

RATATOUILLE

This is one of Patou's and my favorite dishes. Leftovers are even better than the first day's serving.

3 T. olive oil	1 28-oz. can plum tomatoes,
3 medium yellow onions, cut in half	cut up, with the juice
then sliced the long way	1 T. sugar
3 cloves garlic, minced	1 tsp. dried oregano
1 medium eggplant, cubed	1 tsp. dried basil
3 medium zucchini or	1 tsp. salt
yellow squash, sliced	Freshly ground pepper
2 large peppers (red or green),	Parmesan or Romano cheese (optional)
seeded and sliced	

Heat olive oil in a large skillet or Dutch oven over medium high heat. Add onions and allow to caramelize slightly, then add garlic and cook briefly until the garlic is lightly browned. Add the eggplant, peppers, squash, tomatoes and sugar, and stir. Bring to a boil, then lower heat, cover and allow vegetables to simmer for ¹/₂ hour. Check to make sure the heat is low enough and the vegetables are slowly stewing in the tomatoes.

Add the remaining ingredients, taste and adjust the seasonings. Stew for an additional 15 minutes. Top with Parmesan or Romano cheese, if desired. This can be served hot or warm. It is even better a day or two later, by itself or as a filling for an omelet.

Makes 6 to 8 servings

Greens

We Americans don't eat enough greens. I have tons of excuses—they take up too much room in the refrigerator, they take too much time to clean and prepare, and so on. This is the one vegetable that I have to force myself to make. And I do, because greens are wonderful sources of vitamins and minerals.

Many produce markets don't carry them. They deteriorate rapidly and they really do take up a lot of room. Greens should be cooked as soon after picking as possible (there goes the "no room in the refrigerator" excuse).

Fresh local greens hit the market in spring and remain a fixture throughout the summer and fall. If you are going to use them raw in a salad, select the smaller, younger leaves. Young dandelion greens add a wonderful bitterness to otherwise sweet salad greens. The larger leaves can be stir fried or braised.

CLEANING SPINACH

Rinse by submersing 2 lbs. or 3 to 4 bunches of spinach in water and lifting them out. Spinach grows in sandy soil, and you want the sand to fall to the bottom when you lift out the spinach. Rinse until no more sand is removed from the spinach. Dry well.

STIR FRY SPINACH

I love lightly cooked spinach. To make certain I don't overcook it, I have everything else for dinner prepared and ready to eat before I start cooking the spinach.

2 bunches spinach, cleaned with tough stems removed	4 cloves garlic, finely chopped
2 T. peanut oil	1 minced shallot
	1/4 cup chicken broth

Wash and dry the spinach well. Cook the garlic and shallot in the oil until they are slightly browned and the aromas are released. Add the spinach and toss to coat in the oil. Add the chicken broth and cover. Cook 1 more minute. Sprinkle with 1/2 tsp. pepper sherry (optional). Stir to distribute the sherry and serve at once.

Makes 3 to 4 servings

PEPPER SHERRY

I have found the hot sauces add more than heat. The red type sometimes throws off the balance of a dish by infusing too much vinegar, some add too much salt, and still others are so concentrated that they can easily overpower a dish. And then there is Pepper Sherry. Added at the end of the cooking, Pepper Sherry brightens a long simmered soup or stew and adds a depth of flavor to quick cooked foods. I am liable to add it to almost anything, but if you like this, you will find your own uses for it.

1 cup dry sherry
¹/₄ cup clean hot peppers (I use serrano when I can get them)

Combine the 2 ingredients in a clean glass container. Cover and let rest for 1 week (or longer if you really love heat). Remove the peppers and refrigerate the liquid. Use as desired.

Peas

Green Peas
Peas require cool evenings to flourish, so they are only available in spring and early summer. Like most vegetables, they begin to lose their sweetness after they are picked. They should be chilled as soon as possible after you buy them and used within a few days. Look for shiny and firm pods, with small to medium peas. The pods should show no signs of yellowing or dryness. Shell them just before cooking.

Make the time to try fresh peas when they are available. Buy a pound (which will make about one cup shelled) and shell them. The smaller ones can be tossed uncooked into a salad. Cook the larger ones in lightly salted water for about 5 minutes, or until tender. Add them to rice pilaf, stir fries or vegetable pasta dishes.

After you have made fresh peas, sample different types of frozen peas. Knowing what fresh peas taste like will help you select a viable alternative in the frozen food department. Frozen peas are available year-round and are a lot less work.

GREEN PEAS & MINT

1 lb. peas, shelled (about 1 cup)
1 T. butter
¹/₄ cup mint leaves, chopped

Cook the peas in salted water to cover for 5 minutes, or until just barely tender. Drain, and add the butter and mint leaves. Serve immediately.

Makes 3 servings

Snow Peas

Snow peas are one of my husband's favorite vegetables. Buy small ones (because you eat the pods and all, you want the seeds on the small side). Look for light green pods with tiny seeds showing through. The fresh pods will keep a few days in the refrigerator in a loosely closed plastic bag, but they, like green peas, lose their sweetness rapidly.

I have sliced these lengthwise and used them raw in my pasta salad when broccoli was not available, but I use them primarily in my stir fries. For the stir fries, you can blanch them for 2 minutes in rapidly boiling water or microwave them for 3 minutes first. In both cases, rinse immediately in cold water to stop the cooking. When adding them to the stir fry, just warm them up in the pan. If you have to use frozen snow peas, defrost them at room temperature and add at the end of the cooking process just to warm them up.

To prepare snow peas, break off the stem end and if there is a string attached, pull that off the length of the snow pea and discard. Microwave 1 lb. for 7 minutes, or drop the peas into boiling water and cook for 5 minutes.

Tomatoes

Tomatoes are the one vegetable I always grow in the summer, even if it is just a cherry tomato plant in a patio pot (no weeding required). Tomatoes are available in mid-summer and are abundant in the late summer. The first frost ends their season. The big beefsteaks are best purchased at a farmers' market when they are in season. You can get away with buying plum and cherry tomatoes out of season, or trying some of the new imports, especially the new "on the vine" ones that are left on the plant longer to ripen naturally. In the absolute dead of winter, stick with canned tomatoes.

While none of my dogs has liked raw tomatoes, they have always eagerly devoured foods made with cooked tomatoes.

SAUTÉED CHERRY TOMATOES

I created this recipe out of desperation in the middle of winter, when everything else in the market looked inedible.

1 container cherry tomatoes
1 T. olive oil
1 clove garlic, minced

¹/₂ tsp. dried basil or oregano
2 T. Parmesan or Romano
 cheese

Rinse the cherry tomatoes and dry well. In a frying pan large enough to hold the tomatoes in one layer, heat the olive oil over medium heat. Add the garlic and oregano and sauté until the flavors are released. Put in the tomatoes and roll around in the pan to coat with oil. Cook for 1 minute. Turn off the heat and add the cheese. Cover and let the tomatoes collapse and the cheese melt (about 2 to 3 minutes).

Makes 3 servings

🦴 🦴 🦴 🦴 🦴

BROILED TOMATOES

Select medium tomatoes, one per two large dogs or any size person. Slice in half. Top with a little garlic salt, basil and Parmesan cheese. Broil 5 inches at the perimeter of the heat source for 5 to 6 minutes until the tomato is cooked through and the cheese bubbles. (I usually broil these when I am broiling the meat dish. I place them on the edge of the broiler away from the direct heat.)

1 broiled tomato per person

🦴 🦴 🦴 🦴 🦴

Squash

WINTER SQUASH

When you are cooking for only two people, one winter squash can go on forever—unless you share it with your dog.

The two most readily available winter squashes are acorn and butternut. In both cases, look for hard, smooth, blemish-free produce. They store very well for weeks in a cool, dry place.

To prepare the squash, cut it in half and scoop out the seeds. Place, cut side down, in a baking dish large enough to hold them. Pour boiling water into the dish to come ½ inch up the sides of the squash.

Bake in a 375-degree oven for 45 to 50 minutes, or until soft.

Remove the squash from the oven and turn cut side up. Put a pat of butter into the squash and add a tablespoon of either maple syrup or brown sugar. Swirl the butter mixture around the inside of the squash. Let the heat from the squash melt the mixture.

1 squash makes 3 servings

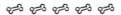

SUMMER SQUASH

While summer squash, including zucchini, are very abundant in the home garden, finding good ones at the market can be trying. Select the bright color, smaller ones, heavy for their size. They should show no signs of wrinkling or bruising. Handle them carefully, and store in a loose plastic bag up to four days in the refrigerator.

Rinse well, and trim off both ends. They can be used in any of the eggplant recipes, including Eggplant Parmesan. Summer squash can also be grilled, brushed first with either olive oil or bottled teriyaki sauce.

If I am doing one of my "it's in the oven" meals, I will start the baked chicken or meatloaf, and 40 minutes before the meat is finished I will put in the summer squash casserole.

SUMMER SQUASH

Summer squash was the first vegetable my kennel dogs ate. It was not a planned addition to their menu.

A wonderful young woman, Lisa Burkhart, lived with Ed and me for a number of years. Lisa and I decided one summer to make pickles, so we planted cucumbers. Two dozen seedlings. The first clue that we were in trouble came when the blossoms were yellow, not white. Then we noticed these bushes had no intention of vining. The blossoms turned to small yellow vegetables. Summer squash.

The early part of the season was fun. We attacked the abundance with gusto. We experimented. We had Summer Squash Parmesan. Summer Squash Ratatouille. Summer squash baked, boiled, steamed and fried. We bartered them for tomatoes and cucumbers and other vegetables. We had tons of all kinds of vegetables that summer.

The dogs got into the act, too. We would steam two or three of these squash and add them to their food. They loved it.

By the end of the season, we were still producing bushels of these golden vegetables daily. We all had had enough of them. Ed, Lisa and I couldn't look at them; the dogs refused to eat them. Our friends and neighbors walked in the opposite direction when they saw any one of us approaching them with a brown paper bag.

Without discussion, Lisa took charge. Every morning she would pick the squash, pack them in brown bags and load them in her car. I accused her of unloading them in unlocked cars at the local mall. She never denied it, but she also never told me what she did with them.

We never mentioned summer squash or cucumbers again. The following year we planted tomatoes, eggplant and peppers.

Variety is truly the spice of life, and too much of a good thing is truly not a good thing.

BAKED SUMMER SQUASH

3 summer squash, cut in 1/4-inch slices
6 plum tomatoes, cut in 1/4-inch rounds
1 medium onion, sliced very thin
1 clove garlic, minced

1 T. olive oil
1 T. fresh basil or 1 tsp. dried
2 sprigs fresh thyme (do not use dried)
Salt and pepper to taste

Preheat oven to 350 degrees. Mix together all of the ingredients. Put in an oven-proof casserole and bake, uncovered, for 35 to 40 minutes.

Makes 4 to 6 servings

🦴 🦴 🦴 🦴 🦴

Chapter 9

Starches Are Staples

Potatoes

There are many types of potatoes available, including some designer varieties that are unusual colors. I basically stay with the russet (or Idaho) for baking, and the run-of-the-mill, all-purpose potato for mashing. When the red-skinned new potatoes are available, I use them for everything.

MASHED POTATOES

My husband Ed hates lumps in his mashed potatoes. He and I have always worked under the assumption that if you don't like the way I do something, it becomes your job. So, this is how Ed makes his mashed potatoes. There are two basic requirements: The potatoes must be fully mashed before any liquid is added; and the liquid must be hot.

6 all-purpose potatoes   1 cup low-fat milk
   (about 3 inches in diameter each)   1 T. butter

Peel and quarter the potatoes. Rinse and put in a pot with enough cold water to cover. Salt the water, cover the pot and bring to a boil. Boil the potatoes gently, about 30 to 45 minutes or until you can pierce them easily with a fork. Do not under cook the potatoes—err on the side of over cooking.

Warm the milk and butter.

Drain the water from the potatoes and mash them well. When fully and completely mashed, stir in the warm milk and butter. Start with $1/2$ a cup of milk and see how moist the mixture is. Add more if you need to, stirring to incorporate the milk.

Makes 4 servings

OVEN-FRIED POTATOES

6 medium baking potatoes	2 tsp. oregano
1 T. paprika	1/2 tsp. garlic salt
1/2 tsp. Old Bay Seasoning	1 T. olive oil

Preheat oven to 350 degrees. Scrub but do not peel the potatoes. Dry well. Cut the potatoes the long way, and slice each half into 3 long, French fry–shaped pieces.

Place in a bowl and mix well with the remaining ingredients. Make certain each potato piece is well coated. Place skin side down on a non-stick baking sheet. Bake 45 minutes, or until the potatoes are fully cooked.

If you're making these with the red skinned new potatoes, cut the potatoes into quarters, and then cut the quarters in half.

Makes 4 servings

POTATO PANCAKES

These are not difficult to make, but they take time and must be made just before eating. They are also fried and I try to avoid fried foods, but sometimes, well . . . . These are just wonderful served with sour cream or apple sauce.

Often when I make these Patou, Ed and I will nibble on them until we are full and bypass whatever else I may have prepared for dinner. This may sound strange, but when I was a kid this was (when we were lucky) Friday night supper.

2 large Idaho potatoes	1/4 cup flour
1 medium onion	Pinch of salt and pepper
1 egg	Oil for frying

Peel and grate the potatoes and the onion. (If I am using my food processor, I will grate the onion at least 1 hour ahead of time. The food processor makes the onion so strong that it needs time to calm down.)

Meanwhile, heat about 1/4-inch of oil in the bottom of a heavy frying pan over medium high heat.

Working quickly, drain any excess fluid from the grated potatoes and onions, then add the egg, flour, salt and pepper, and mix. Drop about ¹/₃ cup of the pancake mixture into the hot oil. Fry until golden. Turn and then fry the other side. Remove to paper towels to drain, and if you can, hide them in a 200-degree oven to keep them warm until dinner.

Makes 12 pancakes (or enough for 2 adults and 1 Great Pyrenees)

Sweet Potatoes

These are new-found treasures for me. I didn't like them as a child and never was tempted to try them as an adult. Then I learned how good yellow and orange vegetables are and sampled one baked in a restaurant. Plain. No decorations, no sweet syrup and, thankfully, no marshmallows. They were wonderful, and I was hooked.

Select sweet potatoes that are heavy for their size and unblemished. Wash them and pierce with a fork. Encase each potato in tin foil. The potatoes vary so much in size and shape that I put them in at least 1 hour before the rest of the dinner is to be finished. I give them a squeeze toward the end of the cooking time; they will give to light pressure when they are cooked through. When done, remove from the oven. They will stay warm in their tin-foil jackets for almost an hour.

Whenever I roast something in the oven, I put in a sweet potato. I store the cooked potato in tin foil in the refrigerator, and at each meal I slice off a piece and add it to the dog food.

Rice

We eat a lot of rice because it is so easy to make. We use it as a bed for our stir fry dishes, and for almost any meal that is served with a sauce. Leftovers are used for Patou's breakfast.

A word of caution: Rice maintains its heat for a long time. If you are going to serve freshly prepared rice to your dog, allow the rice to cool suffi ciently before serving. Stir the rice and test the temperature with your finger to make sure it is cool enough all the way through.

BASIC WHITE RICE

When I was on a fat-restricted diet, I eliminated the butter in the rice preparation and never missed it. And instead of salt I use a bouillon cube. My dog prefers the rice this way.

4¹/₂ cups cold water
2 bouillon cubes
2 cups long-grain rice

Bring the water and the bouillon cubes to a boil over high heat. Add the rice, stir and bring quickly back to a boil. Cover and lower the heat. Simmer rice gently for 20 minutes or until the water is absorbed and the steam has formed "blow holes" in the rice. Remove from heat and let the rice sit covered for an additional 5 minutes.

This recipe makes about four cups of cooked rice. It also multiplies easily, and the precooked rice can be used at later meals or in fried rice.

MICHELLE'S RICE PILAF

My dear friend Michelle gave me this recipe years ago. She said when you have this in the refrigerator, it's like money in the bank.

I have found this to be true, particularly for dogs who want something more flavorful than plain white rice. The chicken broth flavors the rice, and the oil keeps the rice separated. This makes it very easy to reheat in the microwave.

4¹/₂ cups broth, or water and
   2 bouillon cubes
¹/₄ cup fine egg noodles

2 T. butter or olive oil
Vegetable oil
2 cups rice

Bring the water and bouillon or broth to a boil.

In another large, deep saucepan, heat the vegetable oil over medium high heat. Drop in the egg noodles and, stirring constantly, allow them to turn a medium nut brown. Be very careful at this point, because they will burn easily. When the noodles are brown, add the rice and stir to coat with the oil mixture.

Immediately add the boiling broth. Reduce the heat to low and simmer, covered, for 20 minutes or until all the broth is absorbed.

When the broth is absorbed, remove from the heat. Lift the lid and place a clean kitchen towel across the top of the pot and cover again with the lid. Let the rice sit this way for at least 5 and up to 20 minutes. If you need to hold the rice longer, put in an oven-proof dish and keep warm in a 275-degree oven.

For variety, you can add a cup of frozen peas during the last 5 minutes of cooking.

Makes about 4 servings

SPANISH RICE

This was one of the first dishes I learned to make in a high school home economics class. I can't even remember what was in the first recipe, but this is how it has evolved.

5 cups liquid (1 28-oz. can crushed tomatoes and enough water to make up the remainder)
2 bouillon cubes (chicken, beef or vegetable)
2 cups long-grain rice
3 T. olive oil
1 large Spanish onion, cut in 1/2-inch slices
1 medium bell pepper, cored, seeded and cut in 1-inch cubes
2 cloves garlic, minced
1 tsp. oregano
1/2 tsp. ground cumin
Pinch of sugar
Salt and pepper to taste

Heat the tomato, bouillon cubes and water to boiling.

Heat the oil over medium high heat in a large frying pan. Add the onions and let them brown until caramelized. Add the bell pepper, garlic, oregano and cumin. Stir and cook until the aroma of the seasonings is released. Add the rice and stir to coat.

Add the boiling tomato and water mixture. Cover and cook the rice at a gentle simmer for 20 minutes. When all the liquid has been absorbed, remove from the heat and let rest, covered, for 5 minutes.

Makes about 4 servings

Pasta

Sometimes I do not have enough carbohydrates to supplement Patou's meal, so I will make him some pasta. He doesn't know *al dente* from Al Capone, so I short-cut the routine. Bring the water to a boil and add the pasta (elbow macaroni cooks the fastest). Return the water to the boil, stir, cover and turn off the heat. In 15 minutes the pasta will be ready with no extra effort on your part. And if you have fresh green beans, tip and tail them and add them to the water at the same time. They cook about as fast as the elbow macaroni.

PASTA SALAD

My husband doesn't like this salad. I used to make this to take to an event, but then I discovered my dog loves it as much as I do. Now I make it whenever the spirit moves me. Then we both munch on it for a couple of days.

1 stalk broccoli, cut into florets
4 oz. (half a bottle) no-fat or low-fat Italian salad dressing
1/4 cup chicken broth
1 red pepper, cut in julienne strips

2 T. fresh basil, chopped
2 cloves garlic, finely chopped
1 12-oz. box tri-color rotelli pasta
1/4 cup grated Parmesan or Romano cheese

Microwave the broccoli florets for 3 minutes, then rinse under cold water to stop the cooking. Set aside. Mix together the salad dressing, chicken broth, red pepper, basil and garlic.

Cook the pasta according to package directions. Drain and rinse briefly under cold water to stop the cooking. The pasta should still be warm. Do not drain completely, but place the pasta, slightly moist, back into the pot. Add the salad dressing mixture and toss to cover. When cooled to room temperature, add the broccoli. Then toss with the Parmesan or Romano cheese and serve. This is best served slightly warm or at room temperature.

Makes 4 to 6 servings

Crepes

I love just about anything stuffed: peppers, cabbage, dumplings, wontons, tortillas. Learning how to make crepes and stuffing them with ricotta cheese had me in seventh heaven. The young woman who lived with us for years, Lisa Burkhardt, nonchalantly mentioned one night that her mother made crepes for dinner. My interest was piqued. Lisa got the recipe from her mother and a set of instructions, and the two of us were off.

Crepes are so intimidating, and yet they are so easy. And it is the perfect dish to practice on if you share meals with your dog.

CREPE SECRET

The secret, if there is one, to making crepes, is using a heavy pan that will maintain the heat as you move it on and off the heat. And you must take the pan off the heat to move the batter around.

The first crepe is never, never, never useable. Edible, but not useable. And the first time you make crepes, more than the first one will be less than perfect. Lisa and I made three batches before we got the hang of it. All the kennel dogs got a taste of the less-than-perfect crepes for dinner. And we had a simple version of manicotti.

LISA'S MOM'S CREPES

1 cup pre-sifted flour	1$^{1}/_{3}$ cup milk
1 tsp. salt	2 T. melted butter
4 eggs, well beaten	1 tsp. butter

Combine flour and salt.

Combine eggs, milk and butter and add all at once to the flour mixture. Beat until smooth with a hand or electric mixer, or use a blender. Let the batter rest for half an hour.

Heat 1 tsp. of butter in a heavy 6-inch skillet (I use a non-stick pan) over medium high heat. Wipe the pan with paper towel to distribute butter evenly and remove excess.

Using a $^{1}/_{4}$-cup measure, put a scant $^{1}/_{4}$ cup of the batter into the frying pan. Tilt the pan back and forth so the batter covers the bottom evenly. Pour off any excess batter.

Cook about 30 seconds, or until browned lightly on one side. (This side will usually be the more attractive side of the two.) Turn the crepe over and lightly brown the other side. Turn out onto a baking sheet lined with waxed paper. Continue with the rest of the batter.

(If you only have a 10-inch frying pan, this will make 8 large crepes, and most of the ¼ cup of batter put into the pan will be used.)

Makes 16 6-inch crepes

BREAKFAST CREPES

If you are organized enough to make these crepes for breakfast or Sunday brunch, keep them warm in a 200-degree oven.

Drop a teaspoon of jelly into one quarter of the crepe and fold the crepe into quarters. Sprinkle with confectioner's sugar. Or fold the crepes into quarters and drizzle some warmed maple syrup over them.

Grits

Patou and I were introduced to grits early one morning on Interstate 95 headed south for Florida. Ed, Patou and I stopped for breakfast after being on the road for a couple of hours. I ordered a full breakfast of bacon, eggs, grits and toast and ate about half.

The wonderful waitresses (having spotted Patou being walked by Ed) packed my leftovers in a Styrofoam serving container. And thus began Patou's love of grits.

I prepare them according to the package directions, and because time is always short I prefer the "quick" grits. I do decorate them a bit, using bouillon cubes in place of salt and tossing in some garlic powder. Sometimes I'll sprinkle them with a little Romano cheese.

Allow them plenty of time to cool, because they really retain heat. Use your fingers to test for the proper temperature before feeding grits to your dog.

Another plus: Grits reheat well in the microwave oven.

Chapter 10

Condiments and Side Dishes

YOGURT-BASED COLE SLAW

I developed this recipe before the advent of nonfat sour cream, using the yogurt in place of regular sour cream. Nonfat yogurt still has the cultures that are beneficial to a dog's health and ours.

My husband does not like the tart taste of yogurt, so I tame it with powdered skim milk. Because yogurt cultures and tartness vary so much, start with the amount of dry milk given in the recipe, and keep tasting and adding until the tartness subsides or until you like the taste.

¹/₃ to ¹/₂ lb. shredded cabbage
¹/₃ cup nonfat yogurt
1 T. light mayonnaise
2 T. nonfat dry milk

1 T. vinegar or pineapple juice
1 T. sugar or equivalent substitute
   (or to taste)
Pinch of salt

For the dressing, mix together everything except the cabbage. Pour the dressing over the shredded cabbage (I buy the pre-shredded kind with carrots and use ¹/₃ to ¹/₂ the bag). Toss well and serve immediately.

Makes 3 to 4 servings

🦴 🦴 🦴 🦴 🦴

TRADITIONAL COLE SLAW

The original version goes like this.

1/3 to 1/2 lb. shredded cabbage
1/3 cup sour cream (non-fat or
   light is okay)
1 T. light mayonnaise

1 T. vinegar or pineapple juice
1 T. sugar or equivalent substitute
   (or to taste)
Pinch salt

Mix up the dressing and pour over the shredded cabbage. Toss and serve.

Makes 3 to 4 servings

MOM'S CUCUMBER SALAD

My mother used to make this salad in the heat of the summer when cucumbers were at their best. Mom sliced her cucumbers and onions by hand. I use the food processor. It really speeds the preparation, but I am not sure it is as good.

2 cucumbers, peeled and
   thinly sliced
1 medium onion, peeled and
   thinly sliced

1 tsp. salt
1 cup water
1/2 cup white vinegar
1/2 cup sugar

Put the onions and cucumbers in a non-reactive bowl or a heat-proof jar. Heat the salt, water, vinegar and sugar until the sugar dissolves. Pour the liquid over the cucumbers and toss. Cover and refrigerate for 24 hours.

Makes 4 to 6 servings

CRANBERRY SAUCE

This is so simple, but it really elevates a meal into something quite festive.

4 cups cranberries
1 cup orange juice
1 cup sugar

Wash and pick over the cranberries. Mix the berries, juice and sugar in a heavy pan. Bring to a boil. Boil for about 5 minutes or until the cranberries begin to pop. Allow to cool to room temperature, then refrigerate until ready to serve.

Makes 4 to 6 servings

SALSA CRUDA

I did not originally make this for the dogs, but for company or for my fajitas. However, without the jalepeño pepper it becomes a tasty, healthy inducement for the dog who occasionally is a lazy eater, as tomatoes and onions are high on the list of favorites for most dogs. With the lime juice, it easily keeps for a few days in a covered jar in the refrigerator.

I made this salsa once in a food processor. While I knew the food processor beat an onion into a rage, I had not anticipated the effect it had on a jalapeño pepper—ouch!

This is a good thing to keep in mind when you are "improvising" on a recipe or changing things ad lib. The recipe that had a nice tang became absolute fire, and it didn't calm down for about 3 days. Even the human guests sounded the alarm, reminding us to be even more careful when we are trying new recipes for our pets.

1 28-oz. can plum tomatoes, drained, seeded and chopped	2 jalapeño peppers, seeded, deveined and chopped
1 medium onion, cut into a small dice	Juice of 1 lime
	Pinch of sugar
	¼ tsp. salt

Cut the tomatoes, onion and peppers by hand. Mix all ingredients together. Let rest for 2 hours. This salsa will keep covered in the refrigerator for about 5 days.

Makes approximately 2 cups

BAKED MUSHROOMS

This dish always completes our entire family's (canine, too) Thanksgiving menu. It slips in the oven after the turkey comes out to rest.

8-oz. button mushrooms, sliced
2 shallots, minced
2 T. butter

1 T. flour
1/2 tsp. paprika
1/2 cup sour cream (non-fat works fine)

Preheat oven to 325 degrees. Sauté the shallots in the butter until transparent. Add the sliced mushrooms and sauté quickly about 3 minutes, or until the mushrooms are cooked through.

Stir in the flour and paprika and cook for another minute.

Spray a small oven-proof bowl with vegetable spray. Mix the sour cream in with the mushrooms, and pour into the bowl. Bake for 20 minutes.

Makes 4 to 6 servings

Chapter 11

Desserts

I am not a big dessert eater—definitely not because I don't like dessert, but because I like it too *much*. Still, dogs, like owners, must occasionally splurge, so I will show you how to make the meal's finale sparkle with one of these desserts.

FRIED TORTILLAS

Both dogs and humans think this is fun when you have children who can be the runners with the warm tortillas. Feed them first, then put them to work.

1 package large flour tortillas
Vegetable oil

¹/₃ cup sugar mixed with
   1 tsp. cinnamon

Heat enough oil to generously cover the bottom of a cast iron or other heavy frying pan. Add the tortillas one at a time and brown well on one side. (Ed spins them around in the pan as they cook.) When browned on one side, turn over and repeat the process. When finished, place on paper towels to drain. Sprinkle with the cinnamon sugar and serve warm.

For an extra treat, place these on a serving plate and top with ice cream, or for your canine health enthusiasts, low-fat frozen yogurt. If you really want to be decadent, add some hot fudge and nuts and whipped cream and . . . .

Our dogs get it plain with frozen yogurt. The nuts are difficult for them to digest and the hot fudge can cause allergic reactions. Even with this modified recipe, Patou and the others never appear to feel deprived.

LAURALEE'S CHEESECAKE

I never liked cheesecake. Then my one-time college roommate Lauralee showed up at our house with this one. Out of politeness, I ate a piece. Out of politeness, she gave me this recipe. This is not exactly light fare.

Although it was really not designed as dog food, dogs love the flavor of cheese. Using a tiny piece of this as an occasional treat or inducement would not be harmful if your veterinarian has not cautioned you against giving your dog foods that have a high fat content.

Untopped, it can be frozen in individual pieces, wrapped in plastic wrap. It will keep for about a month (if it lasts that long) in the freezer, and will thaw out in minutes.

The crust:

1½ cups graham cracker crumbs
1 T. sugar

5 T. melted butter
½ tsp. cinnamon

Mix these ingredients together and press into the bottom and slightly up the sides of an 8-inch springform pan.

The cheesecake:

3 8-oz. packages of cream cheese, softened (try the reduced fat variety)

1½ cups sugar
5 large eggs
1 T. vanilla

Preheat oven to 325 degrees.

Beat together cream cheese and sugar. Add eggs one at a time, beating well after each addition. Add vanilla and continue beating. Pour the cream cheese mixture into the prepared springform pan.

Bake 1 hour. Turn off the oven and open the door. Allow the cake to remain in the oven for another half hour.

The topping:

The "I don't have time way":

Open a can of cherry or blueberry pie filling. Pour the fruit on top.
The real way:

2 cups pitted cherries, blueberries or other berries
1 cup sugar

1 cup water
2 T. cornstarch
½ tsp. cinnamon

Mix sugar and cornstarch. Add water and mix thoroughly. Mash $1/2$ cup of the fresh fruit. Add this and the cinnamon to the sugar and water and bring to a boil over medium heat. Boil for about 2 minutes, or until the mixture is thickened and clear. Let cool.

Arrange remaining fruit (many dogs love fruit, and it's as good for them as it is for us) on top of the cheesecake. Top with cooled glaze.

PART III

Other Considerations

Chapter 12

The Puppy's Special Needs

Care and Feeding of Your Puppy

Here you are with a brand new puppy whose systems are stressed out with growth, play, vaccinations and so on. Your new puppy has lost the lifelong companionship of perhaps several furry peers, and is now being introduced into a totally new environment.

You are probably planning to change his food, too. Just remember to take it slowly, and allow *at least two weeks* until the switch is complete.

During the process of switching your puppy to natural foods, do not try to rely on your memory for daily changes in the diet. You have enough to remember without this. Jot down the date and what new food, if any, was added on that date. If there was a negative reaction either to eating the food or a later digestive upset, temporarily remove this food from your puppy's diet and try it again a month later.

You may find foods that your puppy will not eat now, and some that he'll never eat. There will also be some foods that cause illness now and will always cause a negative reaction to some degree. You will be able to find suitable substitutes for any individual food that your pup refuses to eat or cannot tolerate.

Start with the sweet tasting vegetables such as sweet potatoes and cooked carrots. Graduate to milder tasting vegetables like green beans and peas. As the puppy gets older, add the cruciferous vegetables like broccoli and cabbage, and the more fibrous ones like corn. And always seek variety but maintain balance.

During this growth stage, you will want to add some supplements to the puppy's daily ration. Ask your veterinarian or the dog's breeder for suggestions on amounts of vitamins C and E, cod liver oil (in capsule form), and multi-vitamins and minerals to add. We are also seeing many new natural supplements on the market. Explore these. Remember, however, that fat-soluble vitamins such as vitamin E should never be given in great quantity, as they are not excreted in the urine.

Avoid any one specific vitamin or mineral except for those listed previously. Many individual vitamins or minerals require other complementary elements in a very specific ratio (such as calcium and phosphorus) in order to be of benefit, and even more importantly, to prevent damage. By the time you study enough to be considered an authority on these vitamins, minerals, combinations and ratios, your puppy will be an adult.

Concentrate on an abundance of good natural foods, emphasize variety, and keep the carbohydrates, proteins and vegetables in balance.

Managing Your Puppy

Your puppy is probably experimenting and pushing all of the limits. Because you will be giving him a variety of foods, your pup will develop definite preferences. You may be tempted to feed these preferred foods exclusively, but don't. Puppies must learn to eat the variety of foods that you want them to eat as adults. This takes a bit of self-control on your part, but the result is a healthier dog, fewer vet bills and a happier owner.

Follow these simple guidelines when feeding natural foods to your new puppy.

1 Always feed your puppy in a place removed from the general traffic.

2 Try to feed at approximately the same times each day.

3 Give your puppy the food and pick up the bowl with any uneaten food after 20 minutes. If there is no competition in the form of another dog in the house, you may need to set a timer for 20 minutes. This will not only remind you, but will soon teach the puppy that the food will be removed when the timer goes off.

4 Don't be conned into adding extra "special" foods to encourage your puppy to eat. Do it once and you are on your way to owning a finicky eater.

5 Don't use food as a weapon. Do not withhold food if the puppy was naughty. *Part of your responsibility as an owner is to provide regular, nourishing meals for your pet.*

6 All dogs have preferences, and so do puppies. My Pyrs have always loved lamb and liver first, followed by beef, turkey, pork and chicken.

Every puppy tries experimenting and pushing all of the limits. This is Cajun at four months old playing with our dinner. (Photo by Ed Boyle)

But we eat a lot of chicken and turkey, and they certainly don't seem terribly upset by this. Perhaps this is what makes the lamb and liver such a treat.

Making the Switch

The following is a recommended timetable for making the switch to natural foods for your puppy. Use this as a guide only. If your puppy is having a difficult time making the transition, slow it down even more.

Even if your puppy is really enjoying the changes, as I suspect it will, do not speed up the process. Take two full weeks to switch to natural foods. You must give your puppy's rapidly changing and growing body the time to adjust to this new change in its life.

Days 1 through 3

You have already changed the water, so don't further disrupt your new puppy's system by immediately changing the diet. Feed your puppy the exact same food the breeder was feeding for at least three days.

Most puppies will be on a chow designed for growing pups, plus a meat mix and some kind of natural calcium supplement in the form of milk or cottage cheese. Continue the ratios, the types and the brands the puppy was fed by the breeder.

All very young puppies should be offered three meals a day. Their stomachs are small and their food requirements are tremendous for their little size.

The following is a typical schedule. Use this as the baseline for all the changes you will make later.

> **Meal 1:** Kibble and meat mix and/or cottage cheese
>
> **Meal 2:** Kibble and meat mix
>
> **Meal 3:** Kibble and meat mix

Days 4 through 6

If, after three days, the puppy appears to have adjusted to its new home, the stools are firm and everything appears normal, you can now start adding natural foods to the diet.

If your puppy is not already eating cottage cheese or yogurt, add this first and serve it with the first meal of the day. If you were serving meat mix with the kibble at this meal, eliminate the meat and substitute the cottage cheese in the same proportion. This is not the time to switch to low-fat products. Your pup needs the concentrated calories and other facilitating properties of the fat right now. So use regular cottage cheese or yogurt; they contain 4 percent milk fat.

Keep Meals 2 and 3 the same as the original diet, and add a small amount of cooked carrots or baked or boiled sweet potatoes to the third meal.

> **Meal 1:** Kibble and cottage cheese or yogurt
>
> **Meal 2:** Kibble and meat mix
>
> **Meal 3:** Kibble, meat mix and sweet potatoes or boiled carrots

Days 7 through 9

Keep Meal 1 the same. For Meals 2 and 3, reduce the canned meat mix by a half and replace it with an equal amount of cooked chicken or beef.

> **Meal 1:** Kibble and cottage cheese or yogurt
>
> **Meal 2:** Kibble, half canned food and half home prepared meat
>
> **Meal 3:** Kibble, half canned food and half home prepared beef or chicken, plus sweet potatoes or boiled carrots

Days 10 and 11

Keep Meal 1 the same. Eliminate all canned meat mix and replace it with meat you prepare yourself, chicken or beef, and add either cottage cheese or yogurt (whatever you didn't feed in Meal 1) in Meal 2. If you feed yogurt in the morning, add cottage cheese at lunch.

Meal 1: Kibble and cottage cheese

Meal 2: Kibble, cooked chicken or beef and yogurt

Meal 3: Kibble, cooked chicken or beef and sweet potatoes or boiled carrots

Day 12

Substitute rice, pasta or another grain product for one-third of the kibble at each meal.

Day 13

Substitute rice, pasta or another grain product for two-thirds of the kibble at each meal.

Day 14

The switch is complete.

Meal 1: Carbohydrates and cottage cheese

Meal 2: Carbohydrates, beef and yogurt

Meal 3: Carbohydrates, chicken and sweet potatoes or cooked carrots

As the Puppy Gets Older

One month into the program, when all systems are stable, begin adding other fresh cooked vegetables to your puppy's diet. Prepare what is in season and fresh. Asparagus, carrots, green beans, wax beans, chard, eggplant, peas, potatoes and all winter and summer squash are good choices now. Twice a week, add the sweet potatoes.

Once a week, add cooked eggs in place of the meat at one meal. They can be either scrambled or poached. Once a month, cook liver for one meal. Because liver can sometimes cause loose stools, feed this with rice.

Maintain your daily log of what the puppy has eaten, in case you see a negative reaction. Dogs are no more physiologically identical than people are. Even dogs of the same breed will have different reactions, but you can

Cajun at five months loves peas and carrots, but won't touch green beans. Even dogs of the same breed will have different taste preferences. (Photo by Ed Boyle)

manage any individual differences by adjusting which natural foods you are feeding your pet.

Months 3 and 4

Continue the regimen you have established. You can now start with some of the various meat dishes you will share with your dog as an adult.

Expand the vegetable offerings. Add corn and the cruciferous vegetables such as broccoli, Brussels sprouts, cauliflower and kale. The kale can be served both cooked and raw. Shred the raw kale and add this, along with shredded carrots, at least every other day, as tolerances will allow. Alternate these with the sweet potatoes.

At One Year

Most of the dog's major growth is done, so the extra calories that come from the whole milk yogurt and cottage cheese can be reduced. Switch your year-old puppy to skim, low-fat or nonfat dairy products.

Begin offering raw green beans as a between meal snack. The puppy is reaching maturity with a strong digestive system and can begin tolerating more raw vegetables and the fiber that comes with them.

Monitor the puppy carefully when giving raw vegetables. Puppies sometimes enjoy them so much that they eat more than they should. If adding these raw vegetables causes your new pup some discomfort, temporarily decrease the amounts and the number of times you feed them.

And although they are still puppies, they can now switch to the maintenance adult diet. The large and giant breeds should continue the cottage cheese with breakfast until at least two years of age, or until the growth period is over (this is breed specific).

Determining the Right Amount to Feed Your Puppy

The nutritional needs of puppies will change dramatically as they grow, causing them to need more food to accommodate their growth spurts. To guarantee adequate food, be flexible with the amounts given. Stay with the approximate balance of 40 to 60 percent carbohydrates/grains and 25 to 30 percent each high-quality protein and vegetables.

Allow your puppy 20 minutes to finish a meal. If your puppy finishes the food in less than 10 minutes, offer more. Remove what is left over after 20 minutes. Puppies, particularly puppies accustomed to natural foods, know better than we do about how much food they need during any particular growth period.

As the puppies get older, gradually feed them fewer meals. Don't arbitrarily cut them back from three meals to two meals to one meal. *Let them do it themselves.* If they routinely begin skipping one meal a day, consider eliminating one meal—usually the second meal of the day is the easiest to eliminate.

Use the hand-eye method of grading proper weight. Visualize a dog's skeleton. Run your hand over your pup's ribs. If you can see the skeletal outline under the coat, your dog is too thin. Increase the daily ration. If you can't *feel* any ribs, your puppy is carrying too much weight. Cut back on the daily ration.

You will handle your puppy daily, and this rib check will become automatic after a while. If you are ever in doubt, consult your dog's breeder or veterinarian for advice on this.

Calcium

As an owner and lover of a large breed (we used to call them giant, but that is no longer an appropriate description for Great Pyrenees in the United States), we are always concerned about calcium intake during the great growth spurts they experience. If you are the proud owner of a puppy destined to be a large adult, you may wish to add more calcium rich foods to the puppy's diet.

Do not be tempted to use calcium supplements. A multi-vitamin is fine, but targeting a particular nutritional need by adding a specific supplement should only be done by someone who is an expert in the field of nutrition. Add calcium naturally in the foods you feed your dog.

FOOD	CALCIUM, IN MILLIGRAMS
Yogurt, low-fat, 1 cup	400
Milk, skim, 1 cup	302
Cheese, cheddar, 1 oz.	204
100% bran flakes, 1 cup with 1/2 cup skim milk	191
Cottage cheese, 2% fat, 1/2 cup	155
Kale, cooked, 1/2 cup	47
Broccoli, raw, 1/2 cup chopped	2

The following is a list of some excellent sources of calcium. These do not require a Ph.D. in nutrition to add to your pup's diet. *But do not substitute calcium rich foods to the exclusion of other foods.* Every addition requires a balance.

Chewable Bones

Bones are one of the great joys of a dog's life. But if improperly chosen, the dog's joys are also its nightmares. Never give your dog poultry or pork bones. They splinter and can cause internal damage to your pet (puppy and adult alike).

Try to get the long beef leg bones. They are sometimes cut into smaller chunks and have marrow inside. They are available in some supermarkets as soup bones or marrow bones. All bones should be broiled or boiled for several minutes before they are fed, to kill any bacteria that may be lurking within.

Bones not only provide a good chewing exercise (and toys), they supply additional calcium and minerals for your puppy. Limit the amount of time you allow the puppy to chew on the bone. This is another situation where a little is good, but a lot is *not* better.

As a conscientious dog owner, you want to be able to take anything away from your puppy or from your older dog. Use these bones as a way of teaching your puppy to relinquish a coveted object to you.

While petting your puppy, ask gently if you may see the bone. This may require a little coaxing, but the pup should eventually allow you to take the bone. Examine the bone in front of your puppy, and then return it to him. When you want to end the puppy's chewing session, ask the puppy to go out or offer another enjoyable distraction. Remove the bone, put it in a plastic bag and place it in the freezer until the next chew session.

If your puppy will not relinquish the bone under any circumstances or even trade it for another goodie, contact your dog's breeder or a knowledgeable dog trainer for advice. A situation like this needs professional help, and the sooner the better.

Proper training of the puppy will allow you to take a bone or other cherished object away from an adult dog. Henry, even as an adult, loves his bone. (Photo by Bill McCaffery)

Chapter 13

The Sick Dog

Care and Feeding of the Sick or Injured Dog

When dealing with a severely injured or desperately ill dog, you must rely on your veterinarian and the relationship you have established with this professional. Once the critical needs of your dog are being addressed, you must prepare yourself to be strong. You need to take control of your voice, your actions and your emotions. Your dog is undergoing enough stress. Do not compound it by making your dog worry about you. If you cannot deal with the situation, then have another family member or friend deal with your dog until you can do so calmly.

Once you are able to be a positive factor in your pet's recovery, do so. Your dog is confused and in pain. Your primary role in this recovery is to reassure, support and love this animal. You must do it with your voice, your touch and your care.

When your dog is seriously ill, you will want to provide a safe, warm haven away from the usual noise and movement of your household. The preferred safe haven for our dogs is where they usually sleep at night, which is our bedroom. When a problem involves a kennel dog and our bedrooms are upstairs, the dog is placed in a room of the house that is off-limits to all other animals.

Phase I—The Fast

Your dog will usually go into a self-imposed fast. This is the body's way of shutting down one part of the working machine to allow another part (the healing mechanism) more latitude. Fasting is a normal animal response to illness, especially when there is a fever. A one- to two-day fast is a fairly normal reaction to an illness.

Watch your dog and allow it to direct the speed at which you reintroduce foods. If the dog wanders into the kitchen while you are making dinner and tries to check out what is on the counter, you have an excellent clue that appetite has returned. Some dogs will be a little more subtle.

Have water available at all times. Use distilled, bottled or filtered water. Avoid tap water and the unwanted chlorine and other contaminants it contains.

If your dog is recovering from surgery, it will be coming out of a period of imposed fasting. Allow necessary time for sleep, and again, keep a fresh supply of good water available.

Phase I—The Menu
Fresh distilled, bottled or filtered water should be available at all times.

Phase II—Breaking the Fast
In both the ill dog and the dog recovering from surgery, the fast must be broken with fluids. My choice was always the broth from homemade chicken vegetable soup. An immobile dog should still be at the veterinarian on intravenous feedings. You cannot do much until your dog can raise itself up on its elbows and lap the offered soup.

Your primary role in your pet's recovery is to reassure, support and love the animal. Patou and the author share a quiet moment together. (Photo by Ed Boyle)

We have had the most success with the broth from chicken vegetable soup, but you can also try vegetable broth or beef broth. You know what your dog would prefer. At this point avoid milk.

Chicken vegetable soup has always served two purposes for me. The broth is used to break their fast, with the chicken and vegetables offered later. But the more immediate effect was on me. Cooking, chopping, tasting and defatting kept me out of the "recovery room" and prevented me from interfering with my sleeping patient.

Your patient needs time to rest undisturbed. As much as your dog needs comfort, love and food, so too is sleep and time necessary to heal the damage. And while you make the chicken soup, your dog gets peace.

Offer the broth every few hours. We want small amounts in the body to slowly ease the system back on track, but never enough to bloat the dog. If the broth has been accepted and tolerated well two or three times, offer the more substantial parts of the soup—the chicken, noodles and vegetables. If this food is being well tolerated and your dog appears to still be hungry, soak a little whole wheat or multi-grain bread in the broth until it's soggy and feed that.

In between the soup, you may want to offer some plain or vanilla low- or non-fat yogurt, topped with a spoonful of honey. Dogs can easily digest this nutritious food. Make sure the yogurt has active acidophilus cultures, which will help restore beneficial bacteria to the lower intestine. This is particularly important if your dog is on antibiotics, because certain antibiotics wreak havoc with the flora of the intestines, both the good and the bad. Yogurt replenishes the good. Feed yogurt and honey daily during the convalescent period. The yogurt provides added protection to your dog's health and the honey provides energy to a tired body.

The first few days of convalescence use all your observational skills to watch your dog's reaction to the food. If your dog devours it and looks for more, increase the amount of food the next time. If your dog refuses a meal, back off for a few hours and then offer something else. Try the beef barley soup, or offer a favorite food.

If your dog has gone through the one- or two-day fast and still refuses all food, contact your veterinarian. There may be another problem that needs to be addressed by a professional.

Phase II—The Menu

Day 1 (offer every few hours)

> Broth from chicken vegetable soup
> or
> Broth from beef barley soup

Day 2 (or, if tolerated, later in Day 1)

Chicken, noodles and vegetables with the broth
or
Beef barley soup solids

Offer any of the following, as the dog responds:

Plain or vanilla low-fat or non-fat yogurt with a touch of honey
Cooked cereal (oatmeal, farina, cream of wheat and so on)
Poached or boiled egg on dry whole wheat toast

Phase III—The Road to Recovery

Your dog is now eating almost normally and is well on the road to recovery.
Try to establish a feeding schedule that will work for you and your pet.

At this time you will want to feed four small meals a day: in the morning, at noon, at 6:00 p.m. and just before bed. If you have to change dressings, give pills, or in some other way upset your dog, you may wish to add a snack of a slice of cheese, or a cracker with cream cheese or peanut butter to lessen the stress and reward cooperative behavior.

Phase III—The Menu

These suggestions have been labeled for meals at different times of the day. Your dog really does not care if breakfast is served in the afternoon or the late-night snack is served in the morning. Consider your schedule and what you have time to prepare and when.

Breakfast

Cooked egg on whole wheat toast
or
Peanut butter on toast

Lunch

Yogurt with honey on dried cereal

Dinner

Solids from beef barley or chicken soup

Bedtime

Cottage cheese on dried cereal

Keep fresh bottled, distilled or spring water available at all times.

These small meals are designed to be prepared quickly and easily, so that you will not hesitate to take the few minutes you need to put them together. You can, of course, become as elaborate as you want. If you are making an omelet for your lunch, make one for your recuperating friend. It will probably be appreciated.

Other foods from your diet can also be used, and don't exclude your dog's favorite foods. If you have a difficult patient, use your pet's sense of smell to your advantage. For dinner serve what you are eating, especially if it has stewed in the Crock Pot all day or baked for a few hours. The scent of a roasted chicken or baked meatloaf can stimulate the dog's appetite and encourage eating. Don't hesitate to roast a head of garlic or fry an onion for this purpose.

One Final Note

The menus and time sequences laid out here are just suggestions. Throughout the healing process let your patient set the pace. If at any time your dog seems stressed by its food regimen, retreat to a previous level, then try again to introduce more substantial foods a few sessions later. Let your dog guide you in the recovery. Working together, you will facilitate the healing process.

As your dog shows improvement and you begin to let your breath out and relax, it is time for some comfort food. Nothing beats macaroni and cheese at a time like this, for you and your dog.

QUICK MACARONI & CHEESE

1 box elbow macaroni, cooked according to package directions	2 T. flour
	1 cup low-fat milk
3 T. butter	8 oz. grated cheddar or jack cheese

Melt the butter in a large frying pan. On a low heat, stir the flour into the butter to form a roux. Make sure to stir constantly or the flour will burn. When the flour is light brown and has formed a paste, add the milk and stir continuously until the mixture thickens, about 5 minutes. Add the cheese. Pour the sauce over the drained hot macaroni and toss.

Makes 4 servings as a side dish

Chapter 14

The Performance Dog

While you may think of Border Collies in herding trials, Newfoundlands in water trials, Weimaraners in field trials or Salukis in lure coursing as the typical performance dogs, there are many other ways a dog can be a performance dog.

Any dog that competes at an event or any activity that requires training, exercise and physical exertion is a performance dog. Some of the more formal events are field trials, the conformation ring and agility or obedience trials, and there are others.

Although each of these events requires different mental and physical abilities, these dogs are superb athletes and all of them should display the result of their owner's care, exercise, training and feeding. Preparation in the form of proper daily nutrition and a sound training program is the foun-dation for every dog's success on the day of competition.

The performance dog has special nutritional needs to supply its periodic and sometimes extensive energy requirements. The basic premises we rely on to keep our house pets healthy are magnified in the performance dog. We will start with the basic grain/carbohydrate, protein and vegetable diet, as outlined in the beginning of this book, but add customized meals leading up to performance events.

We want to fine tune the diet to provide the dog with as much energy as possible on the day of the event. We also want to facilitate recovery and the necessary replenishment of resources after the event. And we want to help our dog recover from the stress of the event. All of this takes planning and preparation.

The dog supplies the ability to learn and the willingness to work. Good competition dogs love what they do, and it is this spirit, unbroken but channeled, that raises these dogs above the average and makes them great.

The mindset, the stubbornness and the single-minded determination of these athletes can sometimes work against their owners. It is up to the owner to call the shots on the training schedules and the feeding regimen, and develop and maintain a program that works for their individual dog.

Good competition dogs love what they do. This is Taylor taking an agility tunnel, directed by owner Stephanie M. Staszak. (Photo by Tobe Saskob)

You will know just by looking at your dog whether or not your feeding program is working. Every performance dog should exude an aura of good health. It should display proper weight, proper muscle tone and a healthy mental attitude. It should be neither too thin, (perhaps implying overwork or inadequate feeding) nor too fat, putting an additional strain on the muscles and skeletal structure of the dog. Its coat should be abundant and healthy, and its eyes should shine.

Learn to use the hand and eye method to gauge proper conditioning and weight, as discussed in earlier chapters. We want the rib cage well covered with muscular flesh, but we still want to be able to feel that the ribs are under there. If you are not sure of the proper weight for your dog, ask a professional. Consult with your regular veterinarian, or if you also use one, your veterinary chiropractor. These professionals will be happy to help you determine the proper weight for your dog. They don't want to see an underfed, overworked dog or an overweight dog at risk of doing permanent physical damage to itself.

Once your dog appears to be in good flesh and well muscled, either by adding flesh or converting the flab to muscle, you may choose to use a scale to more accurately monitor its weight. However, remember that an unconditioned, slightly flabby dog will weigh less than a conditioned, well-muscled dog. Muscles weigh more than fat. So be sure to establish your baseline only when the dog is already well conditioned and well muscled with adequate flesh over the rib cage. Base all weight comparisons on this. But never, never, never stop feeling the rib cage and other parts of your dog's body. This still remains the best gauge of proper weight and muscle condition.

Prepare That Body

For performance dogs, you will want to maintain the basic carbohydrate and protein intake and continue to feed vegetables as outlined in the rest of this book. But because your dog is working, which requires more energy, more food will be required.

If you want to build muscle, you may need to increase the protein intake. Add protein in limited amounts, perhaps 25 percent more protein-rich food each time you increase protein. Protein stresses the excretory systems of the dog and forces all the internal organs to work harder, so always control and limit the protein.

The extra protein is just that—extra, not a replacement for other necessary food products. If your dog begins to leave the grains and vegetables in the meal, back down slightly on the protein. You want your dog to always eat the carbohydrates and vegetables. This presumes that you have tailored the amount to the dog's current needs and that you are preparing well-balanced meals.

You may also simultaneously choose to reduce the training program to free up the resources the dog's body needs to build extra muscle. See the section in this chapter on muscle wasting for more information.

If you are starting with a couch potato, make haste slowly. You cannot expect top performance out of a dog that is unconditioned. The body is not prepared for physical exertion, and the dog could damage muscles and tendons in the process. For an overweight and out of condition dog, slightly reduce (by no more than 25 percent) the protein and carbohydrates in the meals, and add more fresh vegetables. Concentrate on those rich in fiber, such as broccoli and green beans. Make sure a good percentage of the vegetables are served raw.

Cut the Fat

Fat is abundant in the foods we all eat. It is available to varying degrees in meat, as well as in many vegetables such as corn. The good part of fat is that it supplies essential fatty acids and facilitates the use of fat-soluble vitamins. However, this is a case where too much of a good thing is not better. Limit the quantity of fat in the diet, but do not be too restrictive. Cut off the fat you can see on meats and continue to skim gravies. Remember, balance is the key.

You will want to monitor where the fats come from and limit the amount of fat that your dogs eat. There are two primary reasons that we want low-fat consumption for our performance dogs.

- **Fat consumption reduces other food consumption.** While you may assume that you want to supply fat in the diet of animal athletes to increase their caloric intake and available energy sources, this can actually become counter-productive. Fat will quickly satisfy an appetite, and the dog will stop eating before consuming an appropriate amount of protein, carbohydrates and vegetables. This also means the dog will consume less vitamins, minerals and other nutrients needed by the body.

- **Fat decreases performance.** A fatty meal consumed hours before a big event could negatively affect the dog's performance. As the fat circulates in the bloodstream, it makes the heart pump harder. This can diminish your dog's performance on the day of the event. Expect to achieve the best overall performance by feeding a maintenance diet that consists of a well-balanced meal of low-fat, high-quality protein, carbohydrates and vegetables.

Low-Fat Sources of Protein

- Chicken or turkey without the skin
- Bottom, top or eye round beef
- Mild fish such as flounder, sole and halibut
- Lean lamb

- Game, especially venison
- Egg whites
- Low-fat cottage cheese
- Low-fat yogurt
- Low-fat milk

Work That Body

Food is the fuel for your dog's body (and yours). Burning this fuel provides the energy required by the body to perform certain functions. It also supplies the resources to heal, restore and repair muscle tissues.

Our dogs don't grocery shop, and definitely never read labels. So it becomes our job to supply them with the best foods for efficient energy production and for the recovery from this energy producing process.

A muscle cell can get energy by burning the glucose from carbohydrates, the fatty acids from fat, or the amino acids from protein. We want our canine athlete to use the glucose from carbohydrates as the primary energy source and save the fatty acids as a back-up or reserve.

In a well balanced meal, the carbohydrates are available to convert to glucose and then to energy. For the meals prior to an event, we want to make certain there is enough glucose available to take the dog through the entire event without having to draw on the fat reserves.

The Day Before

In order to achieve this, we must do two things. We must rest the dog for 24 hours before the event. Dogs should not be trained heavily during this period, and we may just want to hold one short "remember this" training session, especially if the dog performs well the first time.

Also, for the day before the event, we want to limit the protein and emphasize the carbohydrates. This will supply glucose to the muscles. Serve at least three meals on these pre-event days, and offer high-carbohydrate snacks between the meals.

Morning meal: Cereal and skim milk

Daytime snack: Low-fat cottage cheese and jelly on whole grain bread

Evening meal: Pasta with Meat Sauce or Flash Fried Rice with braised greens or broccoli

PASTA WITH MEAT SAUCE

In the time it takes to boil the water for the pasta and cook it, you can have this meat sauce done.

1 small onion, diced
2 cloves garlic, minced
1 lb. ground turkey or low-fat
    ground beef
1 16-oz. can tomato sauce or
    a large jar of commercial
    spaghetti sauce

1/2 tsp. each oregano and basil
Pinch of fennel seed (optional)
Parmesan cheese

Sauté the onion and garlic together in a small amount of olive oil over medium heat until the onions are transparent. Add the ground turkey and cook it well, breaking it into small pieces. Drain off any accumulated fat. Add the tomato or spaghetti sauce, the oregano, basil and fennel seeds. Cover and simmer on low for 15 minutes.

Serve on top of cooked pasta.

Makes 3 servings

FLASH FRIED RICE

2 eggs, beaten
2 T. vegetable oil
2 scallions (both white and
    green parts), cut to the size
    of peas

1/4 cup peas
3/4 cup roasted pork, thinly sliced
1/2 cup chicken broth
3 T. low-sodium soy sauce
4 cups cooked rice

In a non-stick skillet, fry the beaten eggs in 1 T. oil, without stirring, until set. Invert the skillet over a plate to remove the eggs. Cut into thin strips. In the same skillet, heat the remaining oil and stir fry the scallions and peas until tender, about 4 minutes. Add the soy sauce, chicken broth and pork, and cook 1 more minute. If you have other leftover vegetables such as broccoli, mushrooms or green beans, you can add them now. Add the rice and the egg strips and heat through.

Makes 3 servings

Emphasize the grain products—carbohydrates. Go lightly on the cottage cheese and skimp on the meat in the meat sauce. Carbohydrates are not very satisfying, so your dog will consume more food than if it were eating a normal meal with more protein.

Today's the Day

The morning of the event, serve cooked rice, oatmeal, grits or Cream of Wheat cereal with skim milk and honey. You do not want much bulk in the dog on the morning of the target day.

REMEMBER

We are preparing a physically and nutritionally sound dog for a special event. This carbohydrate diet should not be followed for more than 48 hours and the dog must rest at periodic intervals. The first meal after the event or series of events will return to the regular maintenance diet.

Post-Event Recovery

After the event, we want to make certain the body can recover quickly and adequately. Many performance events span two days or more, so we must take an active approach to restoring the dog's depleted resources.

For a short period of time following the exercise, the body cells will synthesize carbohydrates faster than normal. Make these carbohydrates available. As soon as the dog is settled down and its heart rate and breathing is approaching normal, offer an energy sandwich.

ENERGY SANDWICH

2 slices of whole grain bread   2 T. jelly
¼ cup cottage cheese   1 tsp. wheat germ

Make a couple of these sandwiches and keep them in your cooler for this purpose. Cut these in half or quarters, depending on the size of your dog, and wrap individually. Offer a half or a whole energy sandwich to your dog every 2 hours until the evening meal.

🦴 🦴 🦴 🦴 🦴

If this is the first day of the competition, feed another low protein, high carbohydrate meal. If this is the second or last day of the competition, feed a normal balanced carbohydrate, protein and vegetable meal.

In a Less Than Ideal Situation

To create energy, the dog's body will draw first from the glucose that is available in its food and stored in its muscles. During an extensive event, the dog's body will have to draw on the fat reserves. If a dog does not have sufficient reserves of fat, the body will begin to burn protein. At this point we begin limiting the recovery ability of our dogs. The body needs to keep the protein available for tissue repair.

If the dog is terribly overworked, too-frequently worked, or fed inad-equately, the body will begin drawing upon the muscles themselves for energy. This begins muscle wasting. When we have reached this stage of carbohydrate depletion, the liver begins to convert the muscle protein to glucose. We are now not only destroying the muscle tissue, but also overworking the liver.

When the body is deprived of glucose, the muscles can continue to function for a period of time. However, the brain must have glucose. Glucose deprivation is also known as low blood sugar. This can lead to dizziness,

The more you control the internal and external environment of your dog, the better chance you have to see your dog achieve peak performance. Here's Taylor taking a tire. Owner Stephanie Staszak. (Photo by Tobe Saskob)

mental confusion and overwhelming tiredness, which is nature's way of halting the body to allow the liver time to convert protein to glucose.

A human being will usually have the good sense to stop working before low blood sugar becomes a problem, but our dogs, as dedicated athletes, will usually continue beyond the sensible point. Hunting dogs, in particular,

MUSCLE WASTING

A performance dog must have adequate muscle to achieve and maintain a high level of continued activity and enough reserve to allow for recovery. An overly thin dog cannot do either. Also, a performance dog must cope with the physical or emotional stresses of competition and the added constant exposure to other (sometimes infectious) dogs. An overly thin dog is again at a severe disadvantage. There is much more danger of injury to a thin dog than to a dog with adequate muscle mass. In other words, *thin is not in.*

Muscle wasting occurs when there is not enough protein available for tissue maintenance and repair. If we have a performance dog that is consistently too thin, there are a number of possible, easily correctable causes.

1. You are working the dog too hard. Ease back on the exercise routine by shortening the length of the training sessions or by alternating daily between one intense session and a less intense recovery session.

2. You are not allowing sufficient time for recovery. As a dog exercises, muscle tissue gets damaged. It must be repaired. This requires time. Age is one of the major variables for the time the body needs to recover. As a dog ages, more time is required.

   A puppy may be ready to go again after a short nap, and a two-year-old may need a day. A six- to seven-year-old dog may need two days to recover fully. A 10 year old dog may require additional time. If you exercise your dog without giving its body the time required to do the necessary tissue repair and to recover, you not only cause muscle wasting, but you increase the chance of severe injury to your dog, as well.

3. You continue the exercise regimen when your dog is suffering from an illness or a disease. If your dog is systematically ill, cease all exercise to allow the body to repair itself. Lessen the intensity of the exercise if it is a local injury. When in doubt—STOP! You must allow adequate time to recover from illness.

4. The dog is improperly nourished. The dog should be getting sufficient protein, but it must be in balance with the carbohydrates. When the carbohydrate level is low, the dog's body will use the available protein to make glucose instead of making necessary tissue repairs.

5. You are not feeding your dog enough. This is the most obvious, but frequently most overlooked problem. It is also the easiest to correct. Increase the quantity of the food you feed your dog. Maintain the proper balance of protein, carbohydrates, protein and vegetables. And emphasize fresh, high-quality ingredients.

will continue until they have gone beyond what is safe. Once the blood sugar levels fall into hypoglycemic territory, the dog can become unconscious and must be rushed to an emergency veterinary hospital for glucose injections.

We never want the blood sugar levels to get this low. And while we try to prevent glucose deprivation, sometimes our preparation is inadequate, or there are extenuating circumstances. When you begin to see fatigue or confusion in your dog, call a halt to the exercise—even during a competition. No ribbon or trophy is worth the health of your dog.

When we encounter this unfortunate situation, we can alleviate the dog's physical distress by offering a readily available supply of glucose. Offer your dog an energy sandwich and enforce a period of rest.

Two Very Important Final Notes

1 **To have a great dog begins with preparation.** This preparation starts with shopping, planning and training. But don't forget that last step—the event itself. Leave nothing to chance—assume nothing. Carry your own cooler packed with ice cubes, clean water and energy sandwiches. The more you control the internal and external environment of your dog, the better chance you have to see your dog achieve peak performance.

2 **Every breed is different, and each individual in a breed is different from the others.** Learn to experiment, within limits. Try to establish baselines for performance. Log food consumed and changes in the dog's exercise program and try to correlate these to the performance baselines. The menus and recommendations here are meant only as guidelines. It is your experimentation and fine tuning of the nutrition and exercise program that will help make your dog one of the greats.

Chapter 15

The Older Dog

Care and Feeding of Older Dogs

If you are lucky (and there is a bit of luck in keeping a dog thriving and healthy), you will become the proud owner of an older dog. Throughout the long life of your pet you have managed to keep the pesticides and fungicides to a minimum, provided good water and easily digestible, healthy foods. You have helped your dog's body to extend the anticipated life span. And it is a healthy extension of the dog's life.

By the time your dog reaches old age, you are partners in its care and feeding. You know all of your dog's likes and dislikes. You know if your dog will devour any new or different food offered, or is set on very specific foods or preparations. You will develop a perspective on canine aging different from that of other dog owners.

Your pet, on natural food, will not age as rapidly as a dog on commercial food. Simply by including foods rich in antioxidants, you slow the aging process. When you stop forcing your dog's body to eliminate the fungicides and pesticides and other preservatives and artificial ingredients that are a part of most commercial dog foods, you stop overworking the organs in the excretory system.

But no amount of good luck and good food will keep your pet young forever. Old age will eventually set in, and you will slowly become aware of the differences and difficulties with your older dog.

Every part of the dog's body begins to feel the stresses of aging. The organs lose strength and resiliency and their functioning diminishes. The scourge of old age settles in with arthritic changes and a lessening of the senses of sight, taste and hearing.

No amount of good luck and good food will keep your dog young forever.
(Photo by Ed Boyle)

The older dog requires more recovery time from exercise. While a young dog will bounce back from strenuous exercise with a short nap, an older dog may require one or two days to be ready to go again.

A dog in the prime of life can take many things in stride that may adversely affect the older dog. All systems are winding down. Along with less kidney function and lung capacity, the digestive system is less efficient. Foods that were easily processed and absorbed are less available to your pet with age.

A dog in the prime of life will have digestive juices more powerful than an aging dog. Your older dog may display a lack of interest in raw vegetables and begin to show a discoloration of formerly bright white teeth.

If your dog is healthy and simply old, many of those problems associated with the aging process are mechanical and are due primarily to a decrease in functionality.

As humans age, many lose their sense of taste. Our dogs may also. But a dog's sense of smell is so many times more acute than a human's that even with some loss of taste sensation, the aroma of food can still attract the older dog. And even if the teeth are sound, arthritic changes can affect the jaw, causing difficulty in chewing. Each of these problems can be addressed as they arise.

Mechanical Changes to Help Your Older Dog

🥣 **Elevate the food bowl.** Many owners with giant breeds do this routinely. But as the older dog begins to suffer arthritic changes, a literal pain in the neck can keep your dog from bending over to eat.

Many pet supply houses offer equipment to elevate the food and water bowls. We built our own. My husband took a heavy plastic single step stool and attached a tin pie plate with holes in the center with a stainless steel screw. This pie plate keeps Patou's Pyrex plate and his other ceramic bowls secure and stable.

🥣 **Cut the food into tiny pieces.** For dogs that begin to have difficulty opening their mouths because of arthritic changes, cut the food into pieces small enough that they can be easily consumed. For a very small dog, you may wish to puree the food and serve it as a paste or slurry.

🥣 **Allow the dog adequate time to drink water, or routinely soak its food in water.** The lapping mechanism is less efficient in the older dog. Don't let the dog dehydrate. Make water readily available in the food and as needed throughout the day.

Dietary Changes to Help Your Older Dog

🥣 **Cook foods with a strong aroma and rich taste.** We have to rely more on the sense of smell than any other sense to entice our pets to eat. The smell of spaghetti and meatballs wafts through the house for hours before the meal. And don't for a minute believe your dog isn't aware of what's cooking.

Whenever you use the oven, roast a few heads of garlic in foil to use when you reheat dinners in the microwave. If the quick whiff of the food coming from the microwave is not enough to stimulate the digestive juices, the roasted garlic certainly is.

🥣 **Concentrate on "good for you" foods.** Up the sweet potato ration. While you have the oven on for the garlic, put in those sweet potatoes you may have been forgetting. Now more than ever, your older dog needs the benefits of antioxidants.

If your dog is simply old but is still healthy, many of the problems associated with the aging process are mechanical. Having a veterinary chiropractor make adjustments on a 14¹/₂-year-old Great Pyrenees helps alleviate some of the problems associated with aging. Patou thoroughly enjoys the ministrations of Sue Ann Lesser, DVM, CAC. (Photo by Ed Boyle)

- **Keep up the calcium and protein levels.** Make certain your dog gets extra protein in its later years—unless he has other age-related problems. Keep the basic two parts carbohydrate to one part each protein and vegetables for meals, but supplement at least three times a week with some dairy calcium either in the form of yogurt, skim milk or low-fat cottage cheese.

- **Reduce the raw vegetables.** Your pet may not be interested in eating raw vegetables. This may just be the result of mechanical difficulties. Try adding grated carrots to the food, or sprinkle the top with finely cut up raw greens or chives.

- **Try a high-fiber cereal for breakfast.** With the reduction in raw vegetables, you are eliminating a major source of fiber. Serve the cereal with skim milk, cottage cheese or yogurt, or dry as a snack.

🥣 **Keep fat consumption down.** Continue to monitor the amount of animal fat in your pet's diet. Animal fats are a repository for pesticides, and reducing the amounts of pesticides consumed will reduce the stress on your dog's excretory system. Reducing the amount of fat will usually stimulate the dog to eat more of other foods containing more vitamins and minerals. It also will keep the dog from gaining weight due to decreased activity.

🥣 **Keep up with your supplements.** Continue your pet on Vitamin C. Vitamin E, a multi-vitamin and cod liver oil capsules may also be recommended for as long as your dog will voluntarily consume them.

Consider adding any one of the enzyme-related products on the market that increase absorption of the food eaten. This will help make the nutrients consumed more available to the body.

A recommended daily menu for your older dog may look like this:

Morning Meal

High-fiber cereal with skim milk, cottage cheese or yogurt
or
A repeat of the previous evening's meal

Evening Meal

2 parts complex carbohydrate (pasta, rice and so on)
1 part cooked vegetables
1 part low-fat meat
1 small serving of sweet potato
2 roasted cloves garlic (if food is reheated in microwave)

Weekly Additions of

2 servings grated raw carrot
2 servings chopped raw leafy green vegetables
3 servings yogurt, cottage cheese or skim milk

Monthly Additions of

1 pound of liver, divided into two meals
4 eggs

Before Bed Snack

Cottage cheese, yogurt or skim milk (if not offered at any other time)
Matzo cracker
Thin unsalted pretzels

Some recipes especially helpful in encouraging an older dog to eat are:

Spaghetti and meatballs (hours of cooking)
Meatloaf and mashed potatoes (gentle texture)
Cheese omelet (gentle texture)

And in the Extreme

Living with an old, old dog is like living with the Sword of Damocles hanging over your head. You are waiting for it to fall. And it does, periodically. Your dog will have good days and bad days. On some of the bad days, your

We have shared two lifetimes together. Edward Boyle, Sr., and Patou. (Photo by Ed Boyle)

dog may show no interest in food. And while an occasional fast day is okay for a young dog, we want to limit the number of these days in the older dog. There are no reserves in some of these old dogs, so we have to preserve everything we have.

So pull out all the stops. Based on the premise that there are no bad foods, just inappropriate amounts, we will use some of these foods to pique our dog's interest in food and get over the bad days.

◯ **Fry some bacon.** It takes awhile to cook, and the aroma is absolutely irresistible. After it is well cooked, drain the bacon on paper towels and offer one piece alone. If it is eaten, quickly scramble an egg and put it on a broken up piece of whole wheat toast. Sprinkle another slice of bacon over that. It will probably be eaten.

◯ **Pizza for breakfast.** Patou went through a phase when he turned 14 where all he would eat was pizza. So that was what he got. After a week, he got over it and returned to his normal diet. We would never have accommodated this behavior in a young, healthy dog. We would probably have seen a two-day fast, a short test of wills and back to normal. But at 14 we can bend some rules.

◯ **Cook a favorite meal.** Both my husband and my dog love sweet Italian sausage, and I make it with my spaghetti sauce. I really don't like it, and consider the fat content too high for regular fare. However, it has its place, and in stimulating an appetite it has no rival. And because Patou adores Italian and French bread, the following is one of his all-time favorite dinners.

SAUSAGE & PEPPERS

1–2 lbs. sweet Italian sausage
3 onions, quartered
3 red peppers, cut in
   1 x 2-inch pieces

3 cloves garlic, chopped
¼ cup fresh basil (or 2 tsp. dried)
1 28-oz. can plum tomatoes
Fresh Italian bread

Cut the sausage into 3-inch pieces. Put them into a non-stick frying pan with enough water to cover the bottom of the pan. Sauté over medium high heat until they begin to cook (change color) on one side. Turn the sausage over and cook on other side. Drain any water and fat from the pan and lower the heat to medium low. Pierce the sausages (I use a poultry skewer, but corn on the cob holders will work) to allow the fat to drip into the pan. Let the sausages brown lightly on one side. Turn them over and pierce the other side. Allow the sausages to brown lightly again on this side. When well browned, remove sausages from the pan and drain on paper towels.

Wipe out the pan and heat 2 T. olive oil over high heat. Add onions and sauté until they begin to caramelize. Put in the garlic and basil, and stir until they begin to give off their aroma. Add the plum tomatoes, breaking them up as you add them. Reserve the juice. Add a pinch of sugar and salt.

Return the sausage to the pan and get them settled into the sauce. Place the red peppers on top in a layer. Do not stir them. Cover, reduce the heat and simmer for 30 minutes or until the sausages are cooked through and the peppers are tender. Add the reserved juice, if needed.

For humans: Serve as a knife and fork sandwich between large chunks of Italian bread. Sprinkle with Parmesan cheese, if desired.

For dogs: Cube bread and slice the sausages on top. Cover with peppers, onions and sauce. A little Parmesan cheese is also a nice touch, but it's optional.

Makes 3 or 4 servings

Chapter 16

It Worked for Henry, Too!

Henry lost weight and gained energy when natural foods were added to his diet. (Photo by Bill McCaffery)

Henry walked into our lives when Patou was 13 and had been on natural food for eight years. Henry is a Bernese Mountain dog and was living with Bill McCaffery, a friend of my husband's, while Bill's brother was on an extended business trip. Henry arrived after dinner, but it was obvious he was still hungry. Patou thinks nothing of accepting a treat and then dropping it uneaten. Henry found them all.

Henry was also carrying more weight than he should. So rather than treat him to more "cookies," I gave him some green beans I had purchased that day. His reaction was the same as Patou's was eight years ago: He loved them.

Bill is an avid gardener, so he could see the logic behind an animal's need for growing things such as vegetables. He started including vegetables in Henry's daily meals. And, although Bill never made the complete switch to only natural foods, there were interesting improvements in Henry.

First of all, Henry lost some weight and his energy level increased. His skin also improved dramatically. Before the change in his diet, after petting Henry your hand would be coated with an opaque, somewhat oily film.

Since the addition of natural foods, Henry's coat is as shiny as ever, but the skin is no longer sloughing off these excretions. And Henry doesn't have that famished look in his eyes. Actually, the last time I saw him he refused a piece of broccoli I offered.

Eventually, Bill's brother returned and Henry went home a thinner, happier dog, with a new set of feeding instructions. I have reprinted them here.

DOG DELIGHT MENU

3 small leaves or 2 large leaves
   lettuce **
1/8 cup shredded carrot **
Carbohydrate—spaghetti, rice,
   bread or yams *

Dog food or meat, fish or chicken *
1 T. olive or vegetable oil (or
    5–6 pumps of Vitacoat plus)
1/4 cup water

* Quantity varies, but should equal approximately 2 cups.
** Any veggie can be substituted, cooked or raw—he seems to like them all! Leftovers from human meals also work well. Remove high-fat ingredients first.

Shred lettuce and carrots into a bowl, drizzle with the oil, add carbohydrate and protein foods, add water and mix well. Serve immediately. Makes 1 serving for 1 Bernese Mountain Dog.

                  🦴 🦴 🦴 🦴 🦴

BETWEEN-MEAL SNACKS

Even though between-meal snacks are frowned upon, Henry loves a handful of cereal, such as the store's brand of bran flakes or corn flakes. Between-meal snacks are limited to no more than two per day: one after the second morning outing and sometimes one after the evening walk.

This is a substitute for Milk Bones or any other commercially available dog treat. Bran flakes are very low in fat, contain little or no sugar and, as we all know, contain fiber, which is very healthy for humans and their best friends.

Appendix A

Cost Considerations

I f cost is a consideration in whether to switch your dog to natural foods, please don't let that stop you. The cost of feeding home-prepared foods is about the same as feeding a good quality commercial dog food.

The last year I fed commercial dog food, I calculated the cost as approaching $1.00 per day per dog. Both Cher and Patou were on a premium national brand of kibble and high-quality canned meat that I purchased at a discount pet supply house. Each week they consumed a large (20 lb.) bag of dry food, and seven cans of meat (half a can each for dinner). Excluding treats, their food bill ran about $15 to $20 per week.

At today's food prices, for those meals that I cook specifically for Patou it costs approximately $1.25 a day. If one meal every two weeks is eggs, it's even cheaper.

With a large freezer you can stock up on chicken legs,

Dogs are good for us. Petting them lowers the stress in our lives. Here Kolby visits Alice in her room at the nursing home.
(Photo by Jim Boles)

ground turkey, and bottom round roasts when they are on sale. The cost for packages of ground turkey and frozen beef or pork liver hovers around 99 cents per pound—for pure, high-quality protein.

There are also freebies that just go along with cooking for a larger group. A 10-pound package of rice costs about $1.00 more than a five-pound package. Many stores charge less (between 10 and 40 cents a pound) for larger packages of meat. Many times you can buy a whole chicken for the cost of one or two cut-up breasts. It takes a minute to quarter a chicken; Ed and I get the wings and breasts, the dogs get the legs and backs.

Most heads of broccoli are too much for two people, but not enough for two meals. Patou gets the extra. Sometimes I peel the stalks and cut them into rounds. And he gets the leaves, the most nutritious part of the broccoli. Then there are the tough ends of the asparagus, and the beet greens. These are all excellent sources of fiber as well as vitamins and minerals. And they are not scraps, although they may have not been part of our human family's diet.

If you really have to have green beans, especially in mid winter, vegetables can sometimes be more expensive per pound than meat. But if you eat with the season and make use of good frozen vegetables in the middle of winter, you can get by.

Then there are the "oops" meals. They looked great in the magazine or the cookbook, but somehow they didn't turn out as well as expected. Anyone who experiments with new recipes, new spices or combinations of seasonings is bound to turn up a few of these "oops" meals occasionally. The human members of the family call out for pizza, but the canine member thinks it's fine.

I love cooking for a canine family member who always, *always* appreciates whatever food I prepare!

Appendix B

Just for the Dogs

Although we would like to live in a perfect world, sometimes we cannot share our meals with our pets. Sometimes I make something that I prefer the dogs not eat (like smoked ham), or the food is too expensive (they love fillet of sole and shrimp), or we go out to dinner too often during the week. If I am cooking, our dogs always get a taste of what I make, and when we go out to dinner, I rarely leave without a doggie bag.

But we can cook *just for our pets*. When I do, their meat consists of whatever is on sale—braised, defatted, and if chicken, skinned and boned.

The less tender cuts of meat, like bottom round roasts, I cut into chunks and place in a crockery cooker with water to cover. These become stews with the addition of a couple of carrots, some cloves of garlic, perhaps some barley, lentils or dried beans. The stew gets a few healthy pinches of rosemary, basil, oregano, cumin, bay leaf or thyme—whatever will enhance the basic stewed meat. Herbs fresh from the garden may be added during the last few minutes of cooking. I start these stews on high for 1 hour, then cook on low for 8 to 12 more hours.

I simmer chicken legs (thighs and drumsticks) in water, with carrots and onions, on top of the stove for an hour or so, or bake them uncovered for 1 hour at 350 degrees. I skin and bone them and freeze some of them in serving sizes to use as needed. I sometimes serve the chicken or beef stew with elbow macaroni cooked with some green beans, or, depending on the time sequence, some rice with frozen peas tossed in during the last 5 minutes of cooking time.

And rather than feed the dogs these stews until they're gone, as soon as I get back into the "cooking for all" routine, I freeze the leftovers in serving-size amounts to pull out when I need them. I do the same with chunks of leftover turkey, or chicken pieces that I got carried away with and cooked too many.

These containerized and zip-locked wonders can become "mystery meals" for days you don't feel like cooking. The dogs rarely, if ever, complain.

When I really fail to plan ahead, I head for the freezer where I always keep 1-pound tubes of frozen ground chicken and turkey. I slit the wrapper, and defrost it in the microwave. When completely thawed, I either turn the meat out onto a plate to finish cooking it in the microwave, or put it in a frying pan with an 8-oz. can of tomato sauce. Sprinkle it with a little garlic powder and oregano, and serve over bread, rice, pasta, whatever.

On drastically unreal days, it's the 3-minute cheese omelet over toast.

Index